I BROKE THE CHAIN

I BROKE THE CHAIN

"An American Dream" or the Perfect Lie?

Mari Neli Bejarano Beltran

**BOOK**LOGIX˙
Alpharetta, GA

10 9 8 7 6 5 4 3 2   1 0 0 9 1 4

ISBN: 978-1-61005-528-4

Library of Congress Control Number: 2014918009

Printed in the United States of America

Scripture quotations are taken from the King James Version of the Holy Bible.

∞ This paper meets the requirements of ANSI/NISO Z39.48-1992 (Permanence of Paper)

To my sisters,

No one knows this story better than the four of us—the hardships we endured, the pain inflicted, and the effect these events had on the rest of our lives. Without you, I don't know that I could have survived. I know that this book will be difficult for us all to read, reliving those horrible memories from our childhood. However, I believe sharing our story with the rest of the world will help bring light to those who are dealing with similar situations by opening their eyes and letting them know they aren't alone. I can never thank you enough for all that you did for me, always taking care of your baby sister. I was truly blessed to have you there by my side through those trying times. Therefore, I dedicate this book to each of you. I love you with all of my heart.

"The LORD is my shepherd; I shall not want. He maketh me to lie down in green pastures: he leadeth me beside the still waters. He restoreth my soul: he leadeth me in the paths of righteousness for his name's sake. Yea, though I walk through the valley of the shadow of death, I will fear no evil: for thou art with me; thy rod and thy staff they comfort me. Thou preparest a table before me in the presence of mine enemies: thou anointest my head with oil; my cup runneth over. Surely goodness and mercy shall follow me all the days of my life: and I will dwell in the house of the LORD for ever."

Psalm 23

CONTENTS

PREFACE

Georgia...what?!" I said to my husband after he told me he was being promoted and that the new position was not in Colorado. I was excited but skeptical at the same time. We were separated for sixteen months while he established himself in Georgia and our oldest daughter finished her last year of high school in Colorado. During this time, I wasn't sure what to expect or what God had in store for me. I had formed a very close friendship with a lady that lived in Grand Junction, Colorado. I would often go and visit with her. One day, I told her my life story and how I wanted to write a book about it. She encouraged me to write, telling me that there are people in the world that need to hear my testimony. I told her that as soon as I got to Georgia, I thought I would start. In the summer of 2010, we all moved to Georgia, and through all the moving, finding a doctor, setting up appointments, finding a hair salon, getting registered for school, and taking care of the family, I started writing. I stayed up late every night, faithfully writing my book for three months. However, over time, I started questioning why God had brought me to Georgia, and the excitement of writing my story dwindled. Also, my girls were having a hard time adjusting, which really made things even more difficult. Despite everything, I finished writing, saved it on my USB drive, got my copyright certificate from the copyright office, and put it all away in a safe place.

To make matters worse, I became even more discouraged when I couldn't find a job. Feeling lonely and depressed, I thought I really needed to find a church. Sometimes, when I would be running errands or just driving around, I would pass an Assembly of God church. I grew up in this type of church, and I had been attending an Assembly of God church in Colorado before we moved. So I was excited to see this church. I kept on saying to myself, *I need to go.* It took me a few months, but I finally made the decision and attended my first sermon at the church. I wasn't displeased at all; the church was amazing. Again, I saw how the devil had been discouraging me from entering God's house. He didn't want me to pursue my dreams of publishing a book and writing letters to the facilities I was in to speak to the youth. He especially tried to keep me away from the hair salon.

Since I was in a new state, I had to find a new hair salon to go to. After weeks of searching, I stumbled across a salon by the supermarket one day while on my way to the store. The lady I met there was so amazing. From the moment I met her, she was easy to talk to and very down to earth. She treated me and my girls well, no matter if we were there for a cut or just stopping by to say hi. After about a year, now 2011, my visits to the salon became few and far between. It had been a few months since my last visit. My oldest daughter went in to get her hair trimmed. The lady asked her about me, telling her that I needed to come visit her and say hi. When my daughter told me, I said okay, but then summer came, and we went on vacation. When we got back, my daughters had to start preparing for school. Although preoccupied, in the back of my mind I kept telling myself that I needed to visit the lady who cuts our hair, but something would always end up distracting me, keeping me confined to the house. I continued to attend church and seek God's desire for me. Summer passed, the girls started school, and I was still looking for work. In the beginning of September, my oldest daughter graduated from college. I was very grateful for the one-on-one time I was given to spend with her. One day, we were returning from running an errand, and I told my daughter that I should stop by the hair salon. I walked in, saw that beautiful face which always greeted me, and just started talking to her. We talked about different things and laughed at each other. I think we talked for about twenty to thirty minutes. Close to the end of our conversation, the topic of me writing a book was brought up. I don't remember what led us to talk about my book, but I do know what followed was God's hand leading me and my hair stylist to talk. So I proceeded to tell her I was in the process of writing a book and what I had done already. I told her I wasn't sure what to do next. Basically, I was stuck and naïve to the process of publishing a book. She asked me what the name of my book was and I said, *Broken Chains.* She excitedly told me, "I also have written a book, and I was about to name it *Broken Chains.*" Instead, she named it *The Mercy of God.* She went on to tell me about a local printer called Apex Book Manufacturing, which is now BookLogix. I felt the Holy Spirit, and chills crept down my spine, completely taken aback by our entire conversation. Since that day, things have been moving rapidly. God humbled me yet again, helping me find my chosen path. Why I ended up in Georgia has become very clear to me now, and in the end, I saw the full picture. Never lose hope. Prayer is powerful. Even when you think God is not listening, he is. Have faith and at the right time he will reveal all he has in store for you!

ACKNOWLEDGMENTS

I would like to thank God first and foremost for the ability to endure and survive everything I went through and for giving me the strength to share my testimony with the world. Although I may not always understand the situations you have put me in, I now know that if I have faith and carry love for you in my heart, in the end, you will reveal all that I need to know to understand.

To my husband, Ben, thank you for being my rock. Your words of encouragement have carried me through the hardest of times. Words cannot describe how thankful I am to have a friend, husband, father to our children, and soul mate like you. I love you deeply.

My girls, my angels. I hope one day you will read this book and better understand my love for you. You are one of the reasons I Broke the Chain.

I am so thankful that I found such a dear friend, Cindy. Even though we came from two different worlds, the connection we have found in each other will forever remain dear to my heart. You have been there for me throughout

every step of completing this book. From late-night conversations to quick text messages asking how my book is doing, you have offered your support to me from the start. I believe God led me to you for many reasons, and every day I am grateful: thank you for all that you are.

Mike and Elsa, thank you for being the glue that helped keep my marriage together and never taking sides or being judgmental.

Nacha, thank you for adopting my son and giving him everything I couldn't. Also thank you for helping me through some rough times. I hold a very special place in my heart for you—I love you.

Anthony, this book is also part of your history, and I pray that after reading this you understand even more as to why I couldn't raise you and give you everything that you deserved. I love you more than you'll ever know, and that's why adoption was the best decision I made for you. I love you.

Nancy, I cannot say enough to you. I am so grateful you came home early that day. Without you, I wouldn't have been able to share my story. I don't think you were aware of my mental state; I wanted to die, and I had taken enough pills to do so. I just remember feeling pressure in my head, my ears were ringing, and my heart was pounding. Then, like an angel from above, there you were. Thank you so much.

Mama Carol, who knew the day I walked into that church that you and I would have created such a bond? I love you, and I thank you so much for all the words of encouragement and all the talks. I love you.

Kenyeta, thank you for directing me to BookLogix. I was truly lost and didn't know whom to contact about publishing my book. There was a reason I walked into your hair salon that day.

Last but not least, I would like to thank my publishing consultant Jessica Parker for her undivided attention. Without your help, I wouldn't have found the words to complete my book. I also want to thank Ahmad Meradji and the entire BookLogix team for helping my dreams to become a reality.

NOTE FROM THE AUTHOR

I *Broke the Chain* is a true memoir of my life. All names have been changed from their original form in order to protect the identity of those involved, as well as protect them from those who wish to demean their character based solely upon their actions described in this book.

PART ONE
Broken Chains

"I love you, but I love my natural kids better."
I remember those words like they were being said to me
today.

CHAPTER ONE

Coming to America

I was two years old when I was adopted from Colombia. My mother had twelve children, and she died a few months after she gave birth to twin girls. From what I have been told, it was spinal meningitis that killed her. My father wasn't in good health either; he had tuberculosis and wasn't able to take care of all of us, which is what led my father to make one of the hardest decisions of his life: to place some of the younger children up for adoption. Five of us made it to the United States. The twins were only a few months old at the time and were adopted by another family. As for me, I was adopted by a separate family along with two of my sisters, Juana and Estela. Juana was four, and Estela was six.

By sending us to America, my father had hopes and dreams that we would have a better life than he and my mom did. People from different parts of the world are told fantasy stories about America, but it isn't as it seems. America is viewed as the most perfect place in the world to live, where we are supposed to be free, where children are given the protection and guidance they need, and where no crimes take place. It's like a gigantic house that is surrounded by a white picket fence, and every plant you see is perfect, overflowing with life. The flowers are breathtaking and radiant; the lawn is so green and evenly cut that it resembles a freshly vacuumed, plush carpet. The house displays so much beauty. From the outside, the windows are sparkly, and the structure is kept up to perfection. Then the doors open, and there it is: America, where there is suffering and pain just like any other part of the world. America has the same problems as the rest of the world—murders, hate, deceit, and people destroying lives of the innocent. In addition to this, the children are invisible and are the ones abandoned and abused by the ones they trust will take care of them.

CHAPTER TWO

New Home

B ack in the late '70s and '80s, child abuse wasn't yet in the public eye as it is now. Child abuse was controversial at the time (and still is), but the line between discipline and child abuse had not been established as clearly as the laws read today, which explains why my sisters and I had to endure so much before finding our way out.

From the time I can remember, there was always anger and hate towards the "adopted children" or just "the girls." I don't remember being called by name very often or being referred to as an individual either. My sisters and I were later told by my adoptive dad that he was actually very affectionate towards us girls (in a good way) when we first came to their home. My sisters did verify that he was affectionate towards us. However, my adoptive mom became very jealous and felt that he was showing too much love to us. She felt his love should be reserved for her and their biological children. According to him, that's why he began treating us the way he did. I personally

don't recall any of that affection. Then again, I was two, and I don't have any memories from before the age of four.

Upon arrival, not only were we stripped of our culture, but we were never encouraged to keep up with our native language. In fact, they never told us anything about where we were from. My sister Sook was five years old when she was adopted from Korea. She had been living there for about a year before we arrived. She was ridiculed and beaten by my adoptive parents for speaking Korean—but what did they expect? Juana and Estela were also forbidden from speaking Spanish. I was told that I didn't really talk that much, but that I did say "mango, mango" whenever I was sitting in my high chair. What were they thinking when they adopted us? How we lived through what I am about to tell you is beyond most people's imaginations, including even my own—especially now that I am a parent.

CHAPTER THREE

Their Way of Life

The family that adopted us also had children of their own; they had three boys, Jim, Chris, and Tom, and two girls, Becky and Cassie. Becky lived at home intermittently while we were there, but Cassie did not. She was mentally handicapped and was put into a facility before we were adopted. The boys all lived at home as well. All together, excluding Cassie, there were eight children and my adoptive parents, Roger and Sarah. We were a "family" of ten.

The house we lived in was set close to the road and was yellow with white trim. The front yard was kept very neat and had some small trees planted along the road. I believe it was just for privacy, but regardless, it was well manicured at all times. The sidewalk was lined with rhododendron bushes all the way up to the front door. Rose bushes lined the driveway, and although it wasn't that big, it served its purpose. At the time, the house appeared much bigger than it really was. I discovered this many years later when I went back to see what had become of it. It was a one-level home, and it had three bedrooms and a bathroom on one side of the house and a family room on the other. The dining room, kitchen, laundry room, and living room were in the middle part of the house. The family room had an office with a sliding door, and against one of the walls of the family room was a bunk bed where Estela and I slept. Also, there was a small area with some shelves for books and a room with no door. This was where "the girls'" clothes were kept, as well as another bunk bed where Sook and Juana slept.

In another part of the family room, there was also a bathroom with a toilet and sink. The sink was actually how we kept clean; we were never allowed—or even shown how—to take an actual shower. To dry off, we had a big red towel that the four of us had to share. It seemed as though the family room was once a garage that had been transformed into a living area. We learned quickly with a few good knocks to the head or a nice beating that the family room was our living quarters. Since "the girls" were not allowed in the other part of the house, watching television was out of the question. Lying in bed, hearing the tune for *Love Boat* often made me curious as to what the family was watching, and what that must be like.

We were forbidden to enter any other part of the house unless we were told to do so. As a matter of fact, a board that was a couple feet in length and width had been placed in the doorway that separated our living quarters from the rest of the house. Having the board present really was intimidating. We were constantly being watched by whoever was present in the other side of the house. The board was a constant reminder of how separated we adopted girls were from the rest of the family. When we would want to speak to Sarah, our adoptive mom, we would have to stand at the doorway and call for her. She wouldn't answer right away, and sometimes she never answered at all. The other family members would only stare at us; they just let us call and call for her. Sometimes they would even smile and laugh at us. When Juana would be at the board and call for Sarah, she would be so nervous and scared—not only of the rest of the family, but at how Sarah would respond—she would pee in her pants. Eventually, her nervousness led to other problems, like her picking her eyelashes off. The family would run and tell Sarah, and she would be out there so fast, beating on my sister for picking at or wetting herself. Sometimes all of us were included in the punishment and got beaten. Afterwards, she would go back to her room, close the door, and never ask us what we had needed in the first place. In spite of the group punishment, we never felt anger towards each other. If anything, we hurt for one another and felt sad.

Other times, if they didn't want to see or hear us, they would close the family room door. I preferred to have the door closed; in a weird way, that made me feel protected. It was a relief and a moment where we could breathe and not feel so tense. Though we were shut off from the rest of the family, I didn't mind because I actually felt safe, and nobody was watching us. We actually got excited and felt relaxed. It was like we were in our own world for a few hours or however long they left the door closed. The door was used as a power trip by the family. They would close it any time they wanted, especially when they didn't want certain events seen by us girls. I remember one time when the police and an ambulance came to our house.

Sarah was lying on a stretcher, unresponsive, and paramedics were calling her name. They forgot about the door at first, but when they finally realized it was open, it was quickly closed. It was never clear what actually took place that day. We were aware of when things were not right, but we were always excluded from the situation.

The family room also had a door that led to the backyard where a covered storage area was added to keep boots, shoes, and other supplies. Beyond that was a patio, which was split up into four big squares. A few feet away there was a shed used for storing food, which they kept in big metal garbage cans. I remember the rats constantly making holes in the floor and getting into the food—nasty creatures! I am not a big fan of rats. Anyways, about 100 feet from the shed there was a barn for the cows and horses with a chicken coop attached to the outside. Next to the barn was another covered area for the tools and supplies needed to keep the farm up and running. All this was on a three- to four-acre area. We had three different gardens, a swing set, monkey bars, and an area for ducks. I loved watching the baby ducks. They were so cute, especially when they would seek shelter from the rain. They would go under their mother's wing to stay dry, warm, and to feel that security that every little thing needs. Do you ever stop and think about how animals long for love from their parents just as much as humans do? Sadly enough, animals treat their offspring better than some humans treat each other. The rest of the property was wooded, apart from a huge field off to the side of the house. Needless to say, we had a lot of space, which meant a lot of work for us girls.

CHAPTER FOUR

Survival Instinct

We weren't very big in size, which wasn't surprising since we weren't fed three meals a day. Sometimes we got one or two meals a day. I remember some of the basic meals being oatmeal, open-faced cheese sandwiches, peanut butter sandwiches, spaghetti, soup, and scalloped potatoes. Fruits and vegetables were not served much, if at all. Rhubarb and blackberries, however, were. The rhubarb was mostly grown for jams and pies, but the blackberries were growing wild. Whenever they were ripe and we were told to pick them, we were definitely eager to do as told. We enjoyed it so much we would overstuff ourselves and cause our stomachs to ache. For us though, it was food, and we needed to eat.

Plenty of times we had to fight the family poodle for scraps of food that were thrown on the floor. While they sat at the dinner table in the dining area having a nice meal, we were in the family room, wondering if somebody was going to feed us. Our stomachs would be growling, and I know for me it hurt because I was so hungry. Other times, if we weren't fed, we would eat dog food. I guess you could say it became a common meal replacement.

We tricked our minds into thinking the dog food tasted like real food; that was the only way we could eat it. I was so young when I started eating dog food I can't recall the first time I tasted it. I do remember trying cat food one time because we couldn't get dog food, and it was sour and very fishy tasting. I never ate it again.

One of the jobs we had was to wash the dishes after the family was finished stuffing themselves, which meant crossing the board that separated us from the rest of the house. We learned very quickly to take advantage of that moment. In the cupboard over the washer and dryer there were always about twenty loaves of bread, and from the family room we were able to see the whereabouts of the family members. We learned to send signals to the person washing dishes whenever someone was coming, as well as when it was safe again. Some of the signals were a loud cough, a certain song, or a clapping game. When the coast was clear, the one washing the dishes would take a loaf or two of bread, go out the back door of the laundry room, and place it under the cat house, which was built for our tomcat. Later, one of us would retrieve the bread, pretending as if we were looking for something. If we were not permitted to go outside, we would sneak out the family room door and get it.

We also hid a red, plastic cubby holder under the cat's house. The person washing the dishes would retrieve the cubby, put dried oatmeal and sugar in it, and put it back under the house—sometimes with a loaf of bread, but most of the time it was just the oatmeal mix. If it was too risky or the family became suspicious as to why the door was being opened, then the food was placed in the garbage we took out; that was another way we would retrieve the food.

Then there were nights we couldn't get anything, and we had to salvage whatever scraps we could from the garbage. No salvageable scraps meant resorting to eating dog food. Once we got the food, whatever it was, the routine was that Sook and Estela would take the food and evenly divide it between the four of us. We took the division of food seriously. If it was not divided equally, I had this scream that would bring the entire family running to see what was wrong. I didn't do that too often because then we all would get into trouble. Needless to say, things were always divided up evenly. At an early age, we learned how to survive. It didn't matter what the consequences were; we knew we had to eat and take care of each other.

As we got older, we got wiser, or perhaps we were just desperate; sometimes it's hard to differentiate the two. At times, we were left home alone and thrown a loaf of already-made peanut butter and jelly sandwiches. They closed the family room door, locking us in from the other side. The sandwiches never lasted long, especially if we were left alone for a few days. Eventually we figured out how to remove the door knob and undo the latch, which later became *multiple* latches once they caught on to what we had been doing—they didn't like us sneaking food.

Using the family room door to get into the other part of the house became more and more complicated. They started propping items up against the other side of the door, and even went as far as placing a tall glass vase filled with a beautiful bluish-green liquid against the door. Opening the door and spilling the contents of the vase caused sheer panic the first time it happened, but then we figured out a way around it. We would mix blue and green food coloring to match it with the liquid still in the vase, fill it up with the exact amount of water as before, and place it up against the door as if it never happened. Once we got what we desired from the kitchen, three of us would go back into the family room while the other one closed the family room door, locked all the latches, and replaced the vase. She would then go out the front door, walk around the house, and re-enter the family room through the back door or a window, whichever one was accessible. The rest of us would be waiting, holding our breath, and praying that she wouldn't be caught.

You ever play Russian roulette? Where you only get so many chances before you actually spin that last fatal spin to the chamber with the bullet? Well for me, that's what it felt like. We were not always caught in action, but whenever food came up missing, they figured it was us; we took whatever came our way. Sarah's and Roger's moods that day would decide whether we all got into trouble or just one person, and usually it was a choice between punishing the two oldest ones, Sook or Estela.

The door from the family room eventually became no longer an option. Instead, we started going around the house to the front door, which was occasionally unlocked, or we would go through a window in order to get into the other part of the house. We usually went in pairs at this point. One time, Sook went all by herself and was caught by Jim just as she opened the front door. She came back pale as a ghost and told us she had been caught. The anticipation of the family's return that day was overwhelming.

As soon as they got home, all hell broke loose. We were first sent outside, and the dread of what was going to happen was unbearable. We were already crying and very scared as we waited. They called all four of us into the family room, and Roger and Sarah ganged up on us. They chose the two older ones first. They made Sook and Estela bend over with their pants down to receive the beating. Juana and I were forced to watch, waiting our turn. I remember both of us were shaking and crying so much we couldn't move. They used croquet sticks. That was a long beating—so long that even Roger and Sarah had to stop and take a break only before starting again. By the time they decided we'd had enough, we were weak and shaky. Sook got dizzy and was having a hard time walking. As she walked out the back door, she fell, hitting her chin on a chainsaw. It cut her pretty deep and bled for awhile. She still has a scar from that day. Needless to say, sneaking into the forbidden part of the house was risky, but we had to eat, especially since we were expected to work all day.

CHAPTER FIVE

Manual Labor

The work we were forced to do outside was back breaking. There was a creek in the woods along a trail that was used to ride and train the horses. The horses we had were big horses, and we were in charge of grooming, feeding, and sometimes riding them. Even though horses are powerful animals, they did not escape Roger's abuse. I remember one time Sook was riding one of the horses when it bucked and took off running. The horse ran right under a branch, catching Sook around the neck. She fell off the horse but continued hanging on. We were yelling for her to let go as she was dragged face-first through the dirt. The horse finally stopped after a few painful minutes. Roger got a hold of that horse and kicked the horse on the side over and over again. The horse's eyes were wide, and it was breathing heavily through its nose. I'm surprised it never kicked him back.

To get down to the creek, we had to go down a steep embankment. "The girls" were told to take metal buckets, wheelbarrows, and shovels down to the creek to get gravel, sand, rocks, or whatever the flavor might have been for that day. They used it to fill holes, repair the driveway, or do whatever they could come up with. Sometimes we were told to bring up the sand, gravel, or rock and just place them in separate piles. Now this creek was a good distance away from the house—probably about a mile or so—and not only were we going back and forth from the house to the trail, but we were also going up and down the embankment in order to get from the trail to the creek. We would have to carry the full metal buckets up the embankment repeatedly until the wheelbarrow was full. Once it was full, we had to push the wheelbarrow all the way back up the trail to the house. It was an all-day project, and if it was not finished that day, it would be there waiting for us to finish the next day. Rain, heat, sleet, or snow, it did not matter. "The girls" were expected to work.

Sometimes while we were working down by the creek, we would be called up by Roger and beaten for whatever reason he could come up with. Afterwards, our hearts would be beating so fast, bodies hurting, but somehow we found the strength to continue on. We felt for each other and were sad to see each other get or be hurt. Even though we didn't say it verbally, our hearts broke for each other. I knew that because we wouldn't like to get one another into trouble; if we did, we knew what would happen. Other times, we would hear a crackle in the woods, and looking through the trees, we would see Jim, Tom, Chris, or Roger watching us. I still get the shivers just thinking of seeing those faces among the trees, staring at us with twisted smiles.

The trees came in handy over the years. Sarah had a fireplace she liked to keep going during the cooler part of the year. The men of the house would cut the trees down and into piles of logs. Of course "the girls" were expected to clean and finish up the mess. We would roll and pull the logs whichever way possible towards home. It didn't matter how far into the woods they were; our job was to get them back to the house. Some logs took all four of us to push them up that steep embankment and down the long trail towards home.

Once we reached our destination, we had to chop them up into firewood. The axes we were given were too heavy for our thin, small arms, but we managed. Our hands were true working hands, blistered and calloused. You may ask, *How?* But only God knows that answer! We chopped them up and stacked them neatly into cords of wood between two metal posts. The piles were not to go any higher than the white lines on the post, and it was to be laid out evenly. Then we covered the wood with a tarp and tied it tightly to the metal posts. Sometimes we had to pound stakes at each corner of the tarp and one on each side to prevent the wood from getting wet.

As if that wasn't enough work for four young girls, we also had to keep up with feeding the animals and tending to the garden. All of this was in addition to our household chores. Before we realized it, night would fall, and we would be starving, stomachs growling. Most times we worked all day on empty stomachs. They only fed us breakfast, which usually consisted of oatmeal. After an exhausting day of hauling and chopping wood, we would be so hungry and thirsty. Dog food was often the only thing to eat, and we drank water from the dog's bowl. It wasn't the best meal, but at least it quieted our growling stomachs enough so we could sleep. We had to do what we had to do—we had to survive!

The field beside the house had to be cut and baled. "The girls" were responsible for loading the bales onto a truck, and sometimes we even had to carry them back to the barn where the hay was stacked. I look back now and wonder how we managed to do such hard work—grown men's work—and still remain healthy. We were never really sick, and if we were, we had to manage. There were no sick days at our house. There were only a few times that Sarah actually showed us some affection when we were ill, but that was always short-lived. It seemed as though something would creep into her head; her eyes would go from being warm to icy cold in a flash, and her face would transform to this disgusted and hard look, as if *we* were the illness. Her whole demeanor would change, and we knew what was next. Even if we had a fever and felt sick to our stomach, she would find anything she could get her hands on and beat us. She would use her hands, sticks, belts, and parts of the vacuum cleaner—anything she knew that would hurt. She always came up with lame excuses for why we deserved a beating; it could have been something we did a week ago or maybe as far back as a few months. She would always remember and tell us, "I should have taken care of it then," warning us afterwards, "Wait until your dad comes home."

During the week, Roger was always gone on business trips. So whenever we heard the car pull into the driveway, our hearts would be pounding so fast. We knew what was coming. Sometimes he would walk around the house in a quiet manner, leaving us to anticipate when the beating was coming. He turned it into a sick game. We were the prey and he the hunter. We despised his games, and they could go on for days if he so desired. We would fool ourselves into thinking we had escaped a beating. He was leaving, right? We were not that lucky. He made sure he left us bruised up for awhile.

Not only did Roger beat on us, but he and Sarah would also fight a lot. We would hear them screaming at each other and later see both with bruises. Even the animals weren't safe, as Roger also took his cruelty out on them. Countless times, we witnessed the beating of man's best friend...our dogs. He would kick them until they were limping, hardly able to run away with their tails between their legs. Afterwards, we would try to offer some comfort by petting them, but they would whimper and wince under our touch due to the pain. We had several different types of dogs. I remember two of the Tri-collies, Molly and Buffy, a mother and son. Buffy was still very young and active. He loved to run, play, and chase us around with Molly close behind. She would try to keep up, but her poor body just couldn't take it anymore. Nature eventually took its course and took her from us. I still can hear Buffy's lonely howling at night, and as time went on, the sadder he seemed. One summer day while out of his pen, Buffy took off running towards the road. He ran right in front of a semitruck, killing him instantly. I always wondered if he killed himself intentionally because he was so lonely.

The other dogs we owned at some point or another included a cocker spaniel (I don't remember its name) and a poodle named Podidy—Podidy the Poopin' Dog. She was the inside dog and got the nickname because she constantly had feces stuck to her backside; she also had fleas. Regardless, I loved that dog. She was often a victim of Roger's wrath. Whenever she would see him, she would growl and bite at the hem of his pants. He would pick her up and throw her from the living room into the family room. Sometimes she would hit the wall and then fall to the floor. Other times she would just land straight on the floor. Either way, I would pick her up and hold her shaking body once Roger left the room.

My mind is flooded with memories of our dogs getting hurt because he or she barked or just happened to be accessible for him to take his frustration out on. Since Podidy was an inside dog, she would use the bathroom on the floor of the family room, which was not carpeted, and we would have to clean it up. We used Spic 'N Span and scrub brushes to clean the floor. If Sarah didn't think we were moving fast enough or meeting her expectations, she would shove and rub our faces in the feces and urine. One time the feces burned Juana's face. She was screaming so loudly, and all we could do was watch. The smell of the urine is what I really remember—it burned the inside of my nose, and I remember it dripping into my mouth; that was disgusting. We could wash off our faces when we were done with what we had to do, but we never felt clean.

Regardless of how Roger and Sarah appeared to hate animals, they kept on buying them. One time they brought home two Tri-collies; they were so cute and fat! We named them Lady and Duke. I kind of liked the responsibility of brushing them, feeding and watering them, making sure they were warm enough, and replacing the shavings in their pen if it contained a lot of urine or feces. The pen was not only used to house the dogs, but also us a few times. They would tell us to sit in the doghouse for a few hours, and we would have to drink out of their buckets of water. Thinking of sitting in the dog pen reminds me of the smell of the shavings; I loved the smell. I don't remember who used to deliver the shavings, but we always had a huge pile that was covered with tarp. It was used a lot in the animals' stalls and pens.

The collies were not excluded from the beatings either. Poor things, they were only being dogs, and the bigger they got, the bigger the beatings got, especially for Duke. He barked a great deal. I think that was his way of calling to us, telling us to come and play with him, but we couldn't. We were busy working. As soon as Duke started barking, Roger was hightailing it out the door to shut him up. I watched in horror as he struck him repeatedly with the handle of a shovel. He beat him with that shovel to the point that Duke had fallen down, but he was still trying to fight Roger off. When it was over and done, Roger had the coldest look in his icy blue eyes. Throwing the shovel down and walking back inside, he strutted as if he had just won a battle. We walked over to Duke, and that is when I saw tears. Have you ever seen a dog truly cry? I sure did that day, and it was heartbreaking. I knew that pain all too well. Duke did not have the strength to get up, so we got the wheelbarrow, loaded him in it, and took him back to his pen. I don't remember exactly how long it took, but it was quite awhile before he could walk out of his doggy house to feed himself. We helped by feeding him by hand and bringing him his water. He rewarded us with a lick on the hand. How we learned to be so compassionate is beyond me, but our dogs and other animals were our escape from everything else we had going on. This is how I remembered Roger when he would come home. It would be us or the animals that suffered his rage. Once he was finished making his rounds, he would leave for another business trip and be gone for another week or so, leaving us in the care of Sarah and their children.

CHAPTER SIX

Horrors of Homeschooling

S omewhat surprisingly, we did go to school. We started out in a Christian school. To this day, I remember the song my kindergarten teacher taught us for snack time: "And so I thank the Lord for giving me the things I need: The sun, the rain, and the apple seed; Oh, the Lord's been good to me."

We went to a few schools, and then, for one reason or another, we started being homeschooled. Sarah homeschooled us for a few years, which seemed like an eternity. She definitely took on more than she could handle, and being homeschooled was an absolute nightmare. She started out the mornings in the living room with her reading to us from the Bible, and if we were lucky, children's stories. Then, after singing Christian songs and praying, she sent us back to our desks in the family room. We had the old-fashioned desks where the top opened and the chair was attached to the desk. All of our books and school materials were neatly stored inside the desk. We had LIFEPAC books: Science, Social Studies, Language Arts, Math, and the Bible. She homeschooled us and one of her own sons, Tom. So there were five of us all together.

Tom was allowed to sit wherever he pleased. Although he was big in stature for his age, he was such a baby, always walking around with a blanket. He hardly ever got into trouble, but when he did, she would make sure to take him into a room, shut the door, and spank him. His spankings were a ride in the park compared to what we got, and his cry was annoying and loud. I had no sympathy for him whatsoever. I felt happy whenever he was spanked; I hated him. He was so spoiled, mean, and as far as I was concerned, he could have been hit by a car, and I wouldn't have cared. Tom had caused so much pain in many different ways.

Homeschooling lasted only a few years, and at first, it was okay. We were actually learning what she was trying to teach us, but that came and went as quickly as a cool breeze on a hot summer's day. Her temper would end up getting the best of her, and there were times when she would close herself in her room for the entire day, leaving us sitting at our desks with nothing to do. We tried to stay busy, but eventually our LIFEPAC books became full. At that point, we would erase and rewrite the work we had already done, and sometimes we couldn't even rewrite what we had done because the paper would tear due to all the erasing. I think our reasoning for going over and over the same schoolwork was out of fear and needing to look and feel busy.

When class was in session, she got angry if "the girls" didn't learn as quickly as she liked or if we told her we didn't understand something. Although she would yell and beat us, she would never hurt Tom. Hitting us hard and frequently with her hands or a wooden spoon, she would leave our chins aching and bruised. Sometimes the hits were so hard we would bite our tongues, causing them to swell. Her hands were lethal. She would pinch our cheeks to the point that her nails would be digging into our skin, piercing it, and causing it to bleed. Slapping or pinching the backs of our arms until they were bruised or bleeding was another form of punishment she liked to use.

I didn't know what Sarah was thinking most of the time, but you know the phrase two heads are better than one? Well, she believed it, but in a sadistic kind of way. She liked to grab two of us by the hair, one hand on each side of our heads, and knock them together. I don't know what that was supposed to teach us, but all it did was leave us dizzy, confused, and with a lump on the side of our head.

Tom was always picking on us as well. Some of the things we were taught were never to talk back to him, never speak to him unless spoken to first, and to always respect him. Sarah always said respect your elders, but that didn't apply when it came to him. He was actually Sarah and Roger's youngest child, but because the two that were older than him, Sook and Estela, were the "adopted girls," he held the title of the eldest child at homeschool. He told us all what to do, and we had to listen and comply with whatever he said; if we didn't, we were in for a beating. Being homeschooled really added more fear and confusion to our lives.

I always had a stuttering problem and a tic disorder for as long as I can remember, so words did not flow easily from my mouth, and my body jerked involuntarily. I would slap the side of my leg or make noises with my throat. No matter how hard I tried to stop, I couldn't. I had to squint to see the clock, but eventually I got glasses. They covered most of my face, but at least I could see. Having glasses made a huge difference, and I learned to tell time. It didn't fix my speech or tic disorder though. Not being able to speak right and having a tic disorder really upset Sarah. I would try so hard but would never succeed. I knew that if I did not say it quickly and accurately, then I was going to get it.

The time came for us to learn about Texas and the Alamo, and for some reason, I could *not* say Alamo. Sarah got so fired up that she grabbed a croquet stick and beat my back. I pooped and peed my pants, and she continued yelling, "Say Alamo!" I don't know if I finally said it or what caused her stop, but she finally did. My back hurt so badly. I also stunk, and so I cleaned myself up the best I could in the sink of our bathroom. I don't remember feeling anything besides just physically hurt, and of course relieved she had finally stopped. Going to bed that night was not pleasant. I couldn't lie on my back, and I kept waking up throughout the night in severe pain.

Each of us experienced the wrath of homeschooling one way or another. Tom would make up stories just to see us get in trouble. Other times, he would be the one inflicting the pain. Once, he stabbed my right hand with a pencil, thinking it was funny. Sook got so mad and rushed to my side to remove the pencil and most of the lead. She cleaned my hand and told me to be quiet before we got into trouble. Still to this day, I have a piece of lead in my hand. I catch myself staring at my hand sometimes, and my mind replays that day so clearly. Just like the time my sister Juana got on top of the swing set and was scared to come down. Tom told her to jump and that he would catch her—she believed him. She jumped, and he moved out of the way. She hurt her leg. I don't recall if it was broken, but it was badly injured. That was one of the few times she was taken to a doctor, and she got a cast. He was cruel like that, and he thought it was funny. He hit my sisters as well and called us names. He also came up with the stupidest song, singing that he was an American, and the rest of us were "chinks, spics, injuns, and finks." There was absolutely no sense to his song, just mean words, and we couldn't tell Sarah what he was doing or saying because he would just deny it all and watch us get beaten. That's probably what made him feel like he had more power over us and the right to violate us.

I was about seven years old, sound asleep in my bed, when I was woken up by a tap on my shoulder. When I woke up, I saw this disgusting thing pointing at me with hair towards the base of it. It was Tom who woke me up, and he instructed me to follow him to the office; I did as I was told. He then told me to pet it. All I knew at the time was that it was a body part. I did not know the name of it until later in life when I learned it was a penis. He then told me to go back to bed and not to say a word, and I never did. I didn't understand what was happening or how I was feeling, but I feared him even more from then on. Times like that became more frequent. When everybody was gone, he made all of us get naked, and he would rub on us with his ugly penis and hands and touch us with his naked body. None of us ever said anything because we were the liars, thieves, and the "adopted children." God knows evilness filled that home.

CHAPTER SEVEN

The Pretenders

S peaking of God, we were raised in a church, and every Sunday we would go. Our family looked like the perfect family, and the pastor used our family as an example for his sermons sometimes. Little did he or the church members know, our family was a wolf in sheep's clothing. When we entered those doors on Sunday mornings, they had no clue what we had endured throughout the week or on the way to church: wearing dirty underwear over our heads and being called nasty names like spics, wet-backs, dirty Mexicans, or whatever else came to their minds. The church didn't know that Sarah stayed up late at night, yelling at black figures that she claimed were coming towards her. She would scream: "In the name of Jesus, I rebuke you. Leave this house." This then prompted her to start reciting verses from the Bible. They didn't know that sometimes during the day we witnessed things moving, like the rocking chair rocking all by itself, and she would begin praying and reading from the Bible. As soon as we hit that parking lot, the underwear came off our heads, and the whole mood changed. It was the weirdest thing, and I am not even sure how to explain it. It's like we were transformed into this perfect family that only lasted during the time we were at church. It was our sanctuary every Sunday, walking through those big doors and seeing friendly and soft faces. Then of course, like all good things, there was an end to the peace, and we had to go back home.

Sometimes we had to put the underwear back on our heads and wear it for the rest of the day. On occasion, they would have my sisters wear boxes or plastic bags on their heads. I'm not sure why or where they came up with that idea. Juana had hearing problems, which made it all the more terrifying when objects were put on her head, and she wasn't able to see her surroundings. Some of their ideas were just downright cruel. Who in their right mind thinks like that, gets joy from it, or feels satisfied hurting children—children that they were supposed to love and give a better life to?

The same thing happened during holidays and family gatherings. It was absolutely amazing how all of a sudden the board that separated us from them would disappear. We were all clean, hair washed and done—our hair was always short and permed, so it was easy to maintain—dressed to impress, and looking like one big happy family. Little did the rest of the family know, while Sarah was washing our hair, she would fill up the kitchen sink with water, hold our face down in it, and nearly drown us because we upset her somehow. We feared what she was thinking each time we got our hair washed.

We had a Christmas tree with all the decorations, freshly baked pies, and all the food. Sarah knew how to bake, and she made a lot of food from scratch. At times, we were allowed to help, which was fun until we made her angry. Every Christmas Eve we read from the Bible about the birth of Jesus and sang Christmas carols. Sometimes Roger and Sarah fought because he would be really late and come home with his face all flushed. He appeared to be under the influence of something, which I later learned was alcohol.

Other times, holidays were just celebrated with our immediate family only, and those were not as good of times. We were allowed to sit at the table and eat with the rest of the family, but we had to sit at the far end of the table. The entire meal was soured by disgusted looks from all of them. We would be so happy to be actually eating. We ate like pigs, but that wasn't our fault—even though somehow it was. I don't recall getting too many gifts and definitely not as much as their kids. But we appreciated what we got and cherished it for a long time. Juana got a stuffed pink cat one year, and somehow one of the eyes popped out. So for Christmas they thought it would be funny to give her the eye back wrapped in a box. They all laughed, and she cried. We didn't see the humor in that.

On Halloween, the mood was different as well. We were allowed to go trick-or-treating, and believe it or not, they let us dress up and go with their children. I don't know what happened to all of the candy, and I don't know that we cared; it was just exciting to get away from the house.

Sometimes over the summer one of our cousins would come and stay with us for a few weeks. I once went with my cousin down to the creek, and Tom saw and told on me. I didn't realize I was doing anything wrong, but when I got back to the house, I was told to go and lay down on my bed. I was terrified. I could hear everyone else outside playing, and then it got really quiet; I guess they had gone down to the creek. Roger came walking in and asked me what I was doing down at the creek with my cousin. I told him we were just playing, and he asked me again. I stared at him. I was confused. He slapped my face, pulled me off the bed, and beat me. I had problems walking on my right leg for quite awhile after that. One of the older brothers, Chris, had been gone somewhere for a while, but when he came back home, he noticed me limping. He asked what had happened. I tried to tell him, but our conversation got interrupted. We were always monitored very closely when we were playing with our cousins. It was probably like that for fear that we were going say something that would reveal the family's secrets.

CHAPTER EIGHT

New Torture

The farm was our outlet for staying out of everybody's way. We tried to stay busy at all times, and we were very creative. We cleared out an area and made a stairway out of dirt; we pretended it was our house. The dirt magically turned into sundaes, cakes, mud pies, and so on. Using our imaginations like this was the only form of escape we had from the abuse.

One of the chores we had was to gather the chickens' eggs and take them to Sarah. Sook figured out that we could cook the eggs in a small metal pan on the fireplace, where we would burn stuff that wasn't needed. Now that was a treat and a good source for getting the strength we needed; boy did we need it for everything we had to endure.

I can't remember the exact age they started making us run as a punishment, but the running was torture. It seemed like the older we got, the more we had to run. After working on the farm, the lack of food, and getting beaten daily, this running idea seemed to be the new thing. I remember running so much that our legs felt like they were going to fall off. Sometimes they timed us on how fast we could run around the trail that was made for the horses. Other times, we ran around the patio, and each time we passed Roger and Sarah, we were hit or sprayed with water by their children; the mocking and laughing was humiliating...I hated them so much.

We didn't have running shoes either. Therefore, we ran in whatever we were wearing that day, which most of the time was boots. We didn't have brand-new shoes or clothes. All of our clothes were bought from the Goodwill store, and it didn't matter if they fit us; we had to wear them either way. Some of the pants my sisters wore were big around the waist and so long that they had to roll them up and tie string around the pants to keep them up. The clothes weren't replaced that often, so we made do with what we had.

We weren't a poor family by any means, especially since their children always had nice things that weren't from Goodwill. But our clothes and shoes were always either too big or too small. If we were wearing too small of a boot, when we ran, it would rub so much against our shins that it caused them to bleed. That didn't matter; we had to keep on running. There were times when they would get so busy with other things that they would forget we were still outside running. Like always though, we watched out for each other and figured out how to take breaks without them knowing, acting like we had been running the whole time. Taking breaks became easier the darker it got because we were able to see inside the house through the windows. That way, we knew the family's every move.

CHAPTER NINE

We're Not Alone

I was about eight when Sarah and Roger gathered the entire family together in the living room. Roger told us that he had either raped or molested his own daughter, Becky. The exact wording is unclear, but either way he had done something very horrible to her. He ended the conversation by saying something along the lines of "I'm sorry, and it will never happen again. Not to any one of you." Even though he never raped us, I wonder what he was thinking whenever he would tell us to pull down our pants and bend over while he beat us. Or why I have a memory of lying on my stomach in the front seat on the passenger side of our car that we had when I was a child, alone with Roger. My pants were down, and my head was towards the door while he sat in the driver's seat, eating an ice cream cone...what was he thinking? My sister remembers being naked and standing in front of the family while they all laughed at her. One can only imagine what Roger—or anybody else, for that matter—was thinking!

After Roger confessed to doing something to their daughter, Sarah didn't have much to say. She just sat there quietly, and now that I look back at the situation, it was rather awkward the way she acted. Then we were all dismissed, and it was never talked about again; of course, it was never reported to the proper authorities.

Estela and I, at one point in time, actually got to sleep on the opposite side of the house in Becky's room, and we would be woken up by the sounds of kissing and giggling. We'd wake up to find Jim standing on the bottom bunk rail where Estela was sleeping, kissing Becky who slept in the top bunk. Eventually we were put back into the family room. When Roger and Sarah were gone, Jim and Becky would be in her room with the door locked. Chris would be yelling their names, asking them what they were doing in there, and telling them to open the door. Becky and Jim would also call Sook into the family room sometimes, locking the door behind them. She never said anything to us about it, but our instincts told us something was wrong.

Eventually Becky started running away and wouldn't be seen for a while. She also got into drugs. One evening we were at church, and she got up in the middle of the sermon, said she was going to use the bathroom, and never came back out. Sarah kept asking where she was, and finally we all started searching for her throughout the church. A day or two later, we went with Roger and Sarah to this house, and there was a man sitting in front of it. He was carving something with his knife, and he had a wicked grin on his face. It was almost as if he knew Roger and Sarah. They went inside while we sat in the car, and it seemed like they were in there forever. I don't know what the extent of the conversation was, but we were pretty sure it had something to do with Becky.

One day she came home high on something asking Sarah what love was. She was saying all kinds of off-the-wall stuff. Instances of her running away became more and more frequent. She eventually got pregnant and had a baby boy. I didn't know much about the father of the baby, but I do know he was extremely abusive, and she ended up moving back home with the baby. We were allowed to look at the baby when he was first brought home, but we couldn't touch him. As he got older, he was taught to be mean towards us and never show us any respect at all. My memories of him are vague due to us not being able to interact much with him.

Becky's running away came to an abrupt stop after she became a mom. Becky was also a victim in that household amongst the men, especially Roger and Jim; she had to learn how to survive, and her way was turning towards anybody or anything that she thought would rescue her. The full extent of what Becky had to endure I will never know, but I am sure she had to and still is fighting a daily inner battle because of what she went through in her childhood.

After Becky stopped running away, Sook started running away and hiding in the woods. We had search and rescue, police, neighbors, and whoever else we could get involved helping us look for her. She was gone for about five days. We were so worried about her. It was like a part of us was suffering, and we knew and felt it. On the fifth day, they found her in an abandoned shed deep in the woods. She had eaten poisonous berries and was barely alive.

During the time she was gone, Sarah told quite the story to the police. She put it in their heads that Sook was crazy; she told them that she did all kinds of strange things. I don't know how much of her story they believed, but they didn't seem to question it either. Sook was brought home and had to stay in bed for a few days after. Sarah and Becky took care of her, at least until she was able to get back on her feet. I remember feeling so relieved she was home, even though nothing changed. We continued getting treated like animals, but I felt protected when it was the four of us.

CHAPTER TEN

A Fresh Start?

E ventually we moved several hours away. We had to give our dogs Lady and Duke away. I cried so hard; they had been our companions for so many years. Our other dog Podidy was put to sleep. Sarah cried, which was very strange to see because all we ever saw was her mean side. The tomcat was left behind, and all the other animals were dispersed one way or another.

We moved into a small house at the end of a cul-de-sac. It was a weird location for us because we were used to the farm and all the work that came with it. Now we lived in a house that had a small fenced-in backyard and not much of a front yard. There was a field off to the side of the house as well. We had neighbors, but we couldn't play with their children. In a sense, it felt like a fresh start, but as soon as we felt that way, those feelings quickly vanished.

Chris had gone off to college, but he came home every now and then. In contrast, Jim was lazy and chose to stay at home. All he did was sleep, eat, and be nasty; he liked his porn. I don't recall him working a whole lot. As for

Becky, she was in and out of the picture. Tom, however, was our age, so he was still in school.

The house was a light tan color on the outside, and it had three bedrooms, two bathrooms, a living room, kitchen, a second living room that was used as an office, and a small garage. Our bedroom was very small. In it, we had two sets of bunk beds, a dresser, and a closet. We weren't allowed to leave our room unless we were going outside. Even then, we had to get permission. The garage was another area we could go, but for the most part, we stayed in our bedroom. Their sons' bedroom was next to ours, and Sarah and Roger's room was at the opposite end of the house, connected to the office. Roger was gone much more, and we were actually enrolled in a school. Sarah got a job there, and she kept a close eye on us. Tom, her pet, watched us like a hawk as well.

My older sisters, Sook and Estela, weren't allowed to look at guys or even mention a guy's name. Estela always smiled ever since she was little, and that irritated Sarah so badly that she constantly accused her of thinking nasty thoughts and of being evil. So whenever we started school, her smile was still there, naturally. Thinking she had done something at school that involved a guy, Sarah would tell her to quit smiling and beat her whenever we got home—still never wiped the smile away.

Both Sook and Estela were now of age to work. Sook worked at the daycare in the school, and Estela worked at Wendy's. Neither one of them ever saw their paychecks though. Sarah would cash it, and she would either spend the money on Tom or just give him the money. Unbelievable! My sisters worked their asses off, and he got the money. Tom was so extremely close to his mom that he would sleep with her, even in his teen years; it just wasn't appropriate. We always had a suspicion that something else was happening, but we could never prove anything.

We were familiar with the workbooks we used in school called LIFEPACs. They were the same ones we had when we were homeschooled. It was hard being in school, and I think we were behind; we were never held back though. When it came to doing schoolwork, I just put down whatever popped into my head first, and then I would go back later and correct it. We were supposed to finish all of our work first before we checked it against the answer key. Once we had finished our work, we were to find the answer key for the workbook we were working on from the filing cabinet. Then we had to take our work and the key and grade it on this Bible bookstand that stood in the middle of the classroom and was big enough for six people to be grading their work at once. At least ninety percent of my work would be incorrect, but I learned how to manipulate the situation. I didn't like asking for help, so while I was grading my work, I would either memorize the right answer or sneak a pencil up with me in order to write in the correct answer. Whenever I got caught, Sarah was definitely made aware of it. I would get a spanking or swats, which was what they were called back then, from the principal. Those swats were nothing compared to what I was used to, and it didn't keep me from cheating.

The workbooks were sent home with us so that our adoptive parents could check out the work we were doing and sign off on our homework. Sometimes, we wouldn't be doing well in school and didn't understand our homework, so we would forge Sarah's signature. We may not have been caught right away, but if she happened to look in the book and see that we had signed her name, we had quite the price to pay.

I hid under my bed one time, making Sarah search for me. She eventually found me and told me to come out. When I refused, she went and got a broomstick and started jabbing me with it, yelling for me to get out. I grabbed the broomstick, fighting with her, and she pulled me out. Becky and Chris held me down on a desk while she beat me. Afterwards, they put me in the garage with all the lights off. She took the other children to school and returned home. I was beaten throughout the day by her and Chris. Becky also told me: "You want to fight? Let's fight! You *think* you're tough. I *am* tough!" She held her fist up to my face. At that point, I wasn't intimidated by any of them. While I was pulling on the broomstick, I apparently injured Sarah's arm, or so I was told. Oh, poor thing! I actually felt good about hurting her. I thought she deserved it, but I didn't dare say or show it.

CHAPTER ELEVEN

Runaways

Eventually all of the abuse got to be too much for Juana, and she ran away in the dead of winter. How sad and scared we were. The police were aware that she had run away, and so it came as no surprise to them when they got a call. The details of what exactly happened to my sister when she ran away is very vague, but she was out in the snow then broke into a house to get out of the cold. During that time, she was able to eat, but somehow ended up getting caught when the owner returned home. How freaked out must he have been? I don't recall her ever being taken to the hospital. They just brought her home and let her sleep for a little bit.

Running away was our way of fighting back. Sook got fed up with everything and ran away as well. Except, this time, we knew where she was and provided food to her daily. She stayed in the field across the way from the house, hidden under trees and bushes. Each day when the family would leave, we yelled for her, and she would come running across the field. We would talk to her and give her food. That lasted for about two weeks, and then one day she was just about to return to her hiding spot when Sarah and Tom drove up and saw her. We told her to run, but Sarah ran to the fence, calling for her. She talked so sweetly to Sook and filled her head with lies. She ended up talking my sister into coming home, but we were glad to have her back safe with us: the four of us again.

I'm not too sure about the events leading up to the detective who started coming around and asking questions. He asked to speak to Sook, and Sarah allowed her to talk to him but never alone. Sook refused to talk, and so he gave her his card for her to hold onto, which she did. The day finally came when Sook sat the three of us down, told us she loved us, but that she had to leave. This time she'd had enough; she was seventeen, almost eighteen. I think she held on just long enough, and she couldn't deal with anything anymore. We all hugged her and cried when she left. She crawled out of our bedroom window and took off running down the road; she was really gone for good this time. I know there was some pressure being put on her by that detective. He wanted her to come forward with the events that were taking place at home, but Sook wanted nothing to do with it; I can't say I blame her, fearing the unknown. So she left, and then there were only three of us left to continue with the everyday struggles of our lives.

CHAPTER TWELVE

The Problems Continued

Eventually we moved again. This time we moved out of the city and into the country. Sarah and Roger bought a house that was a two-story home, and, of course, the three of us were put downstairs and not allowed in other parts of the house except to use the bathroom. Not only were we kept downstairs, but we were also put back to work—back to work just like when we lived on the farm. Except this time, we didn't have all the animals. There was a lot of yard to keep up with now, so that kept us busy.

As always, history repeats itself, and the same things started happening again. We were reminded of the fear and pain that was inflicted upon us. Things between Sarah and Roger became very heated, and they started fighting much more. We would be downstairs sometimes wondering if they were going to fall through the floor. Sarah would throw her teacups that she had collected from around the world at him, and they would hit each other. We knew this because later there would be evidence of it, and we could see bruises on their faces.

Roger often received phone calls and always took them in his room, locking the door behind him. Sarah became suspicious and began listening to his conversations. She caught him talking to his secretary once and yelled into the phone, and then she stormed into the room. Needless to say, a huge fight broke out. After that, Roger was gone for quite a bit, and we rarely saw him. When we did see him, he was as cold and cruel as always.

CHAPTER THIRTEEN

Deep in the Woods

When I was eleven years old, I did something that upset Sarah a great deal. I don't recall what got her upset, but I remember her slapping me around; she told me to go back downstairs, and as I was on my way down, she said, "I love you, but I love my natural kids better." I don't know why that hit me so hard, but I stopped dead in my tracks and stared at her through the rail of the stairway, searching her face. All I saw was a cruel witch staring back at me. We stared at each other for what seemed like an eternity, and as she finally started coming towards me, I ran down the stairs. It was like a light bulb came on, and I finally understood what made us so different, why we were treated so differently from her own children. See, we *weren't* her children. We were...*adopted!*

Something changed inside me after that day, and I too started running away from home. I ran with her words in my head, crying. I don't think I cried because of the family but out of anger, frustration, and years of memories instead; years of bad memories flooded my mind. I hated that family. I hated white people, and I was determined to leave home. The first time I ran away, I ran into the woods across the street and sat there quietly until nightfall. I remember being worried about my sisters, but it didn't deter me in any way.

When night finally came, it started raining, and I got up and headed further back into the woods. I don't know how long, but it was quite awhile before I stopped. I came upon a path and walked down it, passing some cows that mooed softly at me as I went by. I kept going until I spotted a trailer off in the distance. It was dark, but I was desperate to get out of the rain. As I was walking towards the trailer, all of a sudden I was stopped dead in my tracks by the sound of a very low growl followed by a deep bark. I tried to see where the dog was, but I couldn't see anything. It moved closer as I got closer to the trailer. This time it was a warning bark followed with more growling. Needless to say, I decided to forget about the trailer and continue walking on.

I came upon a house with the lights on. Since it looked so warm and inviting, I knocked on the door, and a man answered. Staring at me through the rain, I must have been a quite a sight: wet, muddy, terribly skinny, hair all matted. With big brown eyes and holding out a dollar, I asked him if he would let me stay. He gasped and called for his wife, telling her to bring some towels as he motioned for me to come in. The home was so warm and beautiful. The lady came out, and after taking one look at me, tears formed in her eyes as she rushed over to me, wrapping me in towels. They asked me where I had come from and what I was doing out this late at night. I didn't respond. I just stared back at them. All I knew was that I was wet, hungry, and cold.

They offered me some hot chocolate and told their daughter to come downstairs. When she came down, she was smiling but at the same time just watching me. Then she put out her hand, asking me if I wanted to play, and I gladly accepted the invitation, following her to her room. We played for quite awhile, and I felt so warm and happy. Then her parents came into her room and asked me to come with them. As I walked downstairs, I saw a police officer standing near the fireplace. He looked firm but soft at the same time. He asked me my name. I hesitated to answer, and he said, "You must be Mari," to which I replied yes. He went on to question why I ran away.

Stuttering and feeling exhausted, all I could say to him was how much I didn't want to be at home anymore; the people there were mean. He then asked me if by any chance I had a sister who had run away and was making claims of abuse at home as well. I answered yes. He also asked me what had led me to this house. I told him about how I was actually going to the trailer tucked back in the woods when a dog had scared me away, leading me to find the house. He took a deep breath, shook his head, and gently tapped my head with his hat. "That person living there is a sex offender, and he just got out of prison a few weeks ago."

He also said the guy didn't have any animals, let alone a dog. I know what I heard, and it was a bark followed by a deep growl. But the officer said he didn't have any dogs.

What else could it have been? I believe it was God. He made me go the other way.

The officer thanked the kind people, and I shook their hands. They both hugged me. As for the girl, she was sitting on the stairs just looking at me. The police officer took me back home. As soon as we hit the driveway leading up to the house, my heart started pounding. I swear I think he must have heard it. He walked me up to the door where Sarah was waiting, and she put her arms around me, acting concerned. I already knew that as soon as the officer left I was in a whole other world of trouble. Sure enough, he left, and she spared no time. Sarah beat me and pushed me down the stairs where my other sisters were. I was happy to see them, and I slept pretty well that night actually.

CHAPTER FOURTEEN

One More Gone

Estela still had her job at Wendy's, and, seeing that we weren't being fed, she started stealing food for us. She would put it down her pants or wherever she could and bring it home to us. She would tell us to eat and that she loved us. She was able to eat whenever she worked, so she took care of us the best she could. We worried that she would get caught, but thankfully that never happened. While she was gone to work, the two of us left at home—Juana and I—were rarely spoken to, and we had to stay downstairs or outside.

Time went on, and our desire to leave home grew stronger. Our older brother Jim was such a pervert that he often came downstairs where we were sleeping to watch nasty movies. Of course we were curious to see what he was watching, and we often tried to sneak a peek. He would see us and tell us to lie back down. All we heard were noises. He also collected porn magazines.

One day our curiosity got the best of us, and we searched through his room until we found the magazines. We hid them under our mattress, thinking they were safe there at least until we got home from school. When we were picked up from school that day, we sensed danger. Roger had his sunglasses on and was popping his gum like he did when he was about to beat some butt. Sarah, sitting quietly in the front, didn't say a word.

When we finally got home, we ran downstairs and found all of our stuff strewn all over the room. It was then that we realized what was going on and what they had found. We stayed downstairs until they called us upstairs and asked us what right we had taking other people's things. Then Roger took Estela downstairs and closed the door. All I knew was that she was getting beaten hard. I remember her screaming and him yelling. I kept on looking towards the door and then back at Sarah. She said with a smirk, "Don't worry. He isn't going to hurt her." That was a lie. He beat her like never before. She later told us he made her strip down naked and wrap her arms around a supporting beam so that he could beat her; he broke two shovel handles on her. My sister and I also got beaten but not as badly as Estela had.

Later she was in a lot of pain, but regardless, she kept on working and doing what she could to take care of us. Over the next couple of days, her pain worsened, and she was having a hard time hiding it at work. Her manager ended up asking her what was wrong; he was definitely suspicious.

The day finally came when she broke down as well. Through teary eyes, she told us she loved us but that she had to go; she just couldn't take it anymore. She said she didn't want to leave us, but I think that beating was the last straw for her. It was the straw that broke the camel's back, literally. She hugged us, and we all cried as she left for work; we knew she wasn't coming back. She went to work, walked into her manager's office, and lifted her shirt. He was stunned to see her bruised and broken body under her uniform. She said that pictures were taken, and the person taking the pictures got sick—not because of my sister, but because of what was done to her body.

The cops came to the house. I don't know how Sarah knew the police were coming, but she did. Before they showed up, she had a box filled with papers and was frantically burning them, which struck me as something really bizarre. I don't know what type of papers she was burning, but I do know that it was something extremely important. As she franticly burned stuff, she managed to spew out verbal insults at Juana and me. When the officer finally showed up, we were sent downstairs while they talked. That night was an extremely quiet one.

The days that followed seemed to fly by, and my schoolwork continued going downhill. I was caught cheating again, and knowing Roger and Sarah were going to find out, I anticipated what was going to happen. During our very last recess of the day, I ran and hid in some trees that were overgrown near the school. It seemed like an eternity before the bell finally rang, sounding the end of the school day. I waited until dark to emerge from my hiding spot in the trees. I slept in an old bus that had been sitting on the property with flat tires and grass growing around the bottom part of it. I thought about

Juana; she was all by herself now, and I didn't even get to say good-bye. I cried myself to sleep.

I was woken up by students laughing and talking as they passed by the buses on their way to class. I was angry that they were laughing, and I whispered for them to *shut up*. I spent my day in the bus, but I was tired, hungry, and had to use the bathroom. With nowhere to use the restroom, I relieved myself on the floor. At the end of the day, I was ready to get out of the bus, stretch, and try to find some food.

A few weeks before, my friend, my only friend, had given me her number and told me to call her so that we could go to each other's houses. I knew that would never happen, but I went along with it anyway, saying I would call. I kept that number in my pocket and made sure I never lost it. That night, I got out of the bus, stretched, and walked around the backside of the school. There I saw an open window off to the side of the building. I took off the screen, crawled in, and looked around. I was near the kitchen and a phone. I drank some water, and I wanted to call my friend. So I did.

She answered and said, "Mari, where have you been? Where are you?" I told her that I had run away, and I begged her to come and get me. After she agreed, I told her where I would be. Surprisingly, her father brought her to pick me up. She hugged me, asking if I was okay. After telling her I was hungry, they took me to their house and fed me.

I stayed with them for four days, and then her parents explained to me that it wasn't legal for me to be with them without my parents knowing my whereabouts. They told me that they were going to have to call my parents. I begged them not to. I was talking so fast, trying to tell them in a very simple way that I didn't want to go home. I told them that if I did, I would just run away again. My friend's dad eventually called the police.

When they arrived, they sat me down in the bathroom and talked to me. Afterwards, they called Roger and Sarah. I was scared, and I tried to express that to them. I told them a lot of stuff had been going on at home. I only had a few, old bruises on me but nothing fresh. The officers saw all the scars, but there was nothing they could pin on Roger or Sarah. I was also questioned about whether or not I had a sister that had recently run away from home, same as last time. I told them yes. They kept Roger and Sarah separate from me during the interviewing process. They talked to us for quite awhile. Only after fighting verbally with the cops, pleading with them not to make me go back home, my adoptive parents lost the battle. I was placed in foster care!

PART TWO
Different Lifestyles

Had I survived? Was I really being taken from my home and going to a home where there is love? Was I going to get a fresh start? Everything was going to be just fine. That's what I thought as I was being driven to my first foster home. Little did I know the demons that would haunt me, and what was in store for me.

CHAPTER ONE

Another New Home

I was eleven and a half years old now and heading to my first foster home. I was excited and filled with anticipation. I arrived late in the evening. Upon arriving, I was offered food and something to drink, but I declined both. I was exhausted, and thankfully, I was shown to my room which had four single beds. I was told I could take a shower and go to the kitchen if I changed my mind and wanted something to eat. I didn't take a shower or eat. Instead, one of the foster girls loaned me a set of pajamas and told me it was going to be okay. I went to bed, covering my head with a blanket, and cried quietly. It hit me. Three of us had managed to leave home, but there was still one left behind—Juana. I wondered what she was going through, and I prayed that she would be okay. Eventually I fell asleep.

I was woken up by two girls giggling and kissing each other. I was disgusted and just lay still listening to them. The next morning arrived quickly, and that day was filled with several different events. I wanted to start out the morning with a shower, but I didn't know how to start the water. I didn't ask. I just went upstairs where the rest of the family was sitting around the table eating. I was introduced to the rest of the foster kids and my foster dad. There was about eight foster children, including myself, ranging from the ages eight to seventeen. The foster dad was at one end of the table reading the newspaper, and he was actually talking to the kids in the sweetest voice. The foster mom was laughing and bringing breakfast items to the table.

I was a bit shocked by the atmosphere, and I know my foster mom sensed it. She didn't make it obvious though. All she did was pat a seat and smile. I walked over slowly and sat down. I wasn't sure what to do. So she poured my cereal, and the other foster kids helped her serve me. I ate so good...Oh, that food was amazing! I ate quite a bit, and my foster mom made sure of that. Right away after I was done eating, I started clearing the table. My foster dad said, "You don't have to do that. We got it. Go get ready for the day." He had the kindest smile, and even though he was a bigger guy with a full beard and mustache, he still looked kind.

I went downstairs and sat on my bed. I was trying to build up the courage to ask for help with the shower. One of the girls looked mean, but she turned out to be kind; she had been in foster care for a while, and she understood what I was going through. She smiled at me and asked if I was going to take a shower. I nodded yes but didn't budge. She asked, "You do know how, right?" I shook my head no, and she replied, "Oh! Come on. I'll show you." She showed me how to turn the water on, adjust the temperature, shave, use the shampoo and conditioner, and use the body soap with a washrag. I didn't realize how good a shower felt. When I got out and put on clean clothes, I felt fresh and…smelled clean! That day was filled with a lot of how-to lessons, and I never once was hit or yelled at.

I also met my caseworker, and she talked to me for a little bit. The first thing I expressed to her was my concern for my sister, Juana, the one that was left behind. She was honest with me and said that she wasn't sure what she could do for her. She promised that she would try her best to find out the status of my sister. She was an older lady, friendly, motherly, and stern, but she cared about the foster children. Then she talked to my foster mom in private and left after that.

A day or two later, my caseworker picked me up, explaining that we needed to go back to my house to get my clothes and that maybe I could speak with Juana. That blew up in our faces quickly. Tom answered the door and told us that Sarah didn't want to talk to me. I wasn't allowed to get any clothes, and I certainly wasn't allowed to talk to my sister. That was that, and so we left. I was quiet all the way back to my foster home. My caseworker talked to my foster mom for a bit and then told me good-bye. I was extremely sad.

As the days passed, I met with my caseworker frequently. She kept me informed on what was going to happen. She also gave my foster mom clothing vouchers, and we went shopping for clothes. I didn't know the first thing about shopping, much less about being in a store. I stayed close to my foster mom. I actually got clothes too!

Clothes that were mine, and they weren't used, torn, or too big. They were brand-new...*wow*! Once I got home, I put all my clothes away and changed into a brand-new outfit. Then I returned the clothes I had been using to one of my foster sisters who had loaned them to me, and I thanked her.

CHAPTER TWO

Trapped

I was in the foster home for about two months before I finally quit stuttering. When I was with my adoptive family, I always had this dream about a huge boulder chasing me to the edge of a cliff, and all of sudden, I stopped having this dream. My tic disorder started becoming less severe as well. Eventually, it disappeared altogether.

I was taught so much, like table manners and how to take showers, and I was learning to be more independent around the house. I would pull out a bowl from the cupboard, pour cereal into it, pour the cereal back into the box, and put the bowl back. I would also open and close the refrigerator door several times. I stayed in the shower forever just thinking I was cool. I was doing grown-up things! I was very protective of my belongings though, and I had a tendency to be very intimidating to the other children. To me, in my mind, I didn't see anything wrong with my behavior. I thought it was cool to be able to have so much freedom, as well as having control over somebody else for once in my life.

One morning I was in the kitchen trying to make up my mind on what I wanted for breakfast, and I saw from the corner of my eye one of the foster children watching me. I hated being watched or stared at. My memory would always bring up my adoptive family and the way they would look at me. I suddenly felt enraged. I grabbed a knife and made jabbing motions at her. Then I whispered to her that I was crazy, and I cut my finger, laughing. She screamed and took off running to my foster mom's room.

My foster mom came out, asked me what I was doing, and saw my bleeding finger. She sent one of the other foster children to get the first-aid kit. While she was cleaning and wrapping my finger, she gave me a very puzzled look. Trying to talk to me about it, I started humming and kept on laughing. She had to call my caseworker, and she came over right away.

My caseworker sat at the table watching me. She didn't say much, but she did ask me what I was thinking at that moment. I didn't respond. I just stood there staring at her. I felt mean, hateful, and like something out of my control had taken over my mind—I felt crazy! Therefore, she made a few phone calls and told me I was going for a ride with her. I ended up at a mental health facility for some psychiatric testing. I don't remember all the tests, but there were quite a few. The psychiatrist showed me cards with black ink; it wasn't specific pictures, but it was black ink that looked like it had been thrown on there. I made out pictures of my adoptive family being murdered and me killing the psychiatrist and his family. I also was asked the same questions in many different ways, and I was so tired and confused, I believe I just started blurting out random stuff; now that I look back, it made no sense at all.

At the time it made sense to me, but they saw it as displaying anger towards the mental health evaluator, so I was shown to a different room where they left me alone for quite awhile. Then my caseworker came in and told me that it was probably a good idea for me to stay for some additional testing, which could take up to twenty-four hours. So for that night, I could voluntarily stay at the hospital. I agreed and was led into a locked unit that had other children. I looked around as soon as I walked in, and I noticed a room off to my left with two chairs, a couch, and an office. The office had a window that looked out to all areas of the unit. There was also a men's and a women's restroom. The unit had walk-in bedrooms without any doors and one huge room in the middle of the unit that had been split up into a living room, play area, and dining area.

I was shown to my room, which had two beds. I went and laid down on one and covered my head. There were no doors, and the only privacy you had was when you went to the bathroom. I don't know how long I had been lying down, but I was woken up by a voice telling me to come out and have dinner. I refused and lay there listening to the other children. Their topics were interesting. Some of the kids were crying, which made me mad to hear. I clenched my fists under the blanket, thinking the staff was making them cry. I wanted to punch the adults. I hated them! Although I didn't know them, I still hated them.

Getting up, I walked over towards the doorway of my room and just stood there, observing what was going on. I saw a staff member in the corner with a kid that was crying, and I watched that situation very closely. I felt sympathy for the child, but I felt outraged towards the adult. I saw Roger, not a staff member. I froze. I couldn't move, and I was feeling such rage, but I was snapped out of my gaze when someone called, "Mari, come and eat. Dinner is almost over." I walked over to the table, sat down, and ate a little bit, even though I wasn't hungry. That night went smoothly, and I went to bed, but I couldn't sleep well. My mind was flooding with bad thoughts, memories, echoes of children crying, but most of all I was thinking of my sister who was still at home.

CHAPTER THREE

Going Crazy

Eventually morning came, and the unit was filled with the hustle and bustle of everyone taking showers. Some children were refusing to get out of their beds, and others were cussing and singing. Then breakfast came, and most of the children disappeared. I guess they went to school or whatever appointments they had, but all I know is that I was alone with maybe two other kids. They were sitting quietly at the table playing games. That morning dragged on.

In the afternoon, I was walked down to an office and was met by a different person. He was talking to me and asked me questions about my age, if I knew where I was, and other random questions. I just remember him looking at me—not smiling and writing on a pad—and then I was sent back to the unit. I had no clue what was going on, but I did know twenty-four hours was almost up. I wanted out. I asked the staff if they could call my caseworker to come and get me, but they wouldn't give me a straight answer. Inside my head I was bursting with so many emotions; I was feeling outraged, like a ticking time bomb ready to explode. All I knew was that I couldn't stand the noises and the people. The unit was locked down, so it's not like I could just walk outside any time I wanted to. Then on top of all that, I was losing hope that my case-worker was going to show. Why the hell would she come anyways; nobody else cared—why would she? Finally, she showed up, sat me down in the visiting room, and said that some more tests needed to be done, which could take up to three days. I asked if that meant I had to stay there. She said it was up to me, but she thought it was for the best. She gave me a small bag of clothes and told me she would see me in about three days.

One of the staff members took me outside for some fresh air and also let me play PAC-MAN and Donkey Kong. At least I was able to get away from everybody for a few hours, but then it was back inside. I walked around the gym, picked up a ball, and started shooting it at the hoop. A staff member told me it was time to go back to the unit. I ignored him and continued shooting hoops. He made it very clear that if I didn't go with him at that moment, then he wouldn't bring me back out for the rest of the time I was there. I turned around and acted like I was going to lunge at him. He jerked, throwing up his hands in defense. I laughed so hard, but he obviously didn't. He, on the other hand, was calling for help over his walkie-talkie.

Soon a female staff member came out, and she told me in a firm voice to put the ball down and get back inside. She said that dinner was ready and everybody was waiting to eat. Her firmness made me mad—who did she think she was, telling me what to do? I hated her. In my head, I was thinking of how to hurt her, but I figured she wouldn't touch me—she was scared. I continued shooting hoops, turning around only to smile at them. The type of smile I gave was not nice; I felt like it was evil and powerful. They exited the gym quietly, keeping a close eye on me from the doorway. I eventually put the ball back, turned off the light, and walked inside. The male staff member told me I that I had made a good choice, and he thanked me for finally coming back into the unit. I told him it was only because I wanted to and not because he told me to. He replied, "Okay, Mari. That's fine."

My behavior kept me in the unit for the next three days. One of the other kids taught me how to shuffle cards and play board games. I did art activities and read books. The staff did try to keep us busy. During those three days, I felt like my brain was in a whirlwind, and I was feeling outraged and not happy. I, of course, managed to keep it all inside. So you know how they say actions speak louder than words? Well it's true, and the adults around me saw it. By the third day, I was feeling very agitated, and I began demanding to leave. I told them I was allowed to leave because I stayed voluntarily and they couldn't keep me against my will.

I was right to a point, but if they had seen any behavior that was questionable or that suggested that I wasn't stable, which I wasn't, they could keep me by doctor's order. Some man came into the unit, sat down on the couch, and started observing me as I paced around the unit. He wrote stuff down on pad of paper. He never said anything to me. He just watched. I felt caged and like I had no control. My blood began to boil, and I felt like lashing out at anybody that got in my way. The man eventually left. I continued pacing and not talking to anyone. Thinking about Juana, I wondered if she was okay. I began to feel sick to my stomach, and I started tearing up. I tried to fight back the tears because, damn it, nobody was going to see me cry! Walking into my room, I lay down, covered my head with my blanket, and cried. I heard the scuffle of feet approaching my doorway. I knew it was a staff member coming to check on me. I learned to cry quietly so that nobody would ever know when I was crying.

I fell asleep from exhaustion, and when I did wake up, I heard the other children. They were coming back from wherever they had been all day. I woke up angry and hated hearing the sounds of the other children. I managed to hold it together and join the rest of the group. I waited for about thirty minutes and asked if my caseworker was going to come pick me up. I was told she would be in shortly, and she arrived about fifteen minutes later with the man that had observed me earlier that day. I knew as soon as they walked into the unit and told me to come with them to the visiting room that it was not good news. I followed them and stood in the room. My heart was already pounding, and I felt pissed off. My caseworker, I believe, sensed my agitation and asked me how things were going. I clenched my jaw together so tight that it hurt my teeth, but I didn't stop; the pain was relieving to me. I had my hands behind my back, clenched into fists. My fingernails, the little bit that I did have, were cutting into my skin. Again, I noticed how good the pain felt. My caseworker told me in a mellow voice that she thought it was best that I stay for another week. She explained that I was displaying an array of different behaviors that were concerning to all of the people that had been watching me. I just stared at her. She tilted her head, expressing that look of concern, and she sat there saying nothing, waiting for me to respond. I just continued staring at her, and then I asked if she was done. She nodded. I didn't say good-bye or anything; I just walked out of the visiting room, realizing how quiet it was.

The other children had been taken out of the unit, and there were about three staff members sitting on the couch. I went directly to my room and heard the door to the unit open and then close. My caseworker had left, and so had the doctor. I actually felt sad. I felt like she had turned against me and hated me, tricking me all the while. I felt abandoned. I stood at the window in my room, looking up to the sky: so many childhood memories. Nobody understood what was playing in my mind. Nobody knew what I had been through or the heartache I carried with me. Tears were rolling down my thin face, and not a single staff member cared to ask me if I was okay. They just sat on the couch, talking and laughing. *Assholes!* I thought to myself, *How dare they laugh while I'm hurting!* I flipped them off, stuck out my tongue, and held up my scrawny fist to them, but they couldn't see it because I was in my room.

Two of the staff members left after about an hour, and I figured out that they were there because they thought I was going to freak out about having to stay. So they were the backup. I tried to go to bed, and covering my head, I lay there wide-awake. I don't know what time I finally fell asleep, but I woke up in the middle of the night. I saw that the light from the staff's office was on, and the other lights around the unit were turned on low, which were always turned on low while the children were sleeping. The lights were kept on for safety purposes, not only for the residents but also for the staff. I didn't sleep well that night, so when the morning came, I was tired. I got up anyways, following the routine.

That week I was so busy between appointments, visiting with my caseworker, and all the tests they were running that I felt overwhelmed. These things kept me off the unit for a great portion of the day. Days came and went, and before I knew it, my caseworker had come to pick me up; I was leaving the facility. I was happy but scared at the same time. I don't know where that fear came from, but it was there nonetheless. I returned to my foster home, but it didn't feel the same. I felt like the outcast, and I quickly reacted to what I was feeling by disrespecting my foster parents. It was such a blur for me; I don't remember all the details, but I do remember telling my foster parents no and shut up. I just wanted to do my own thing. They did tell me that if I didn't behave I couldn't live there and continue to disrupt the other foster children. I didn't care and told them to move me. Three days later, I was moved to a different foster home.

CHAPTER FOUR

Defiance

The new foster home they sent me to was the same one that had dealt with my older sister, Estela, who had left our adoptive home when she was sixteen. Anyways, she was placed in this foster home. I was told by my new foster mom that Estela was no problem at all, and she enjoyed having her. I was happy to hear that, especially since I hadn't heard from or seen my sister since she left home. I never knew what happened to her after that day she told us she wasn't coming back.

My stay at this foster home didn't last long either. I was only there for two days before I ran away with another girl. I don't know where we were running to, but all I knew was that we filled each other's heads with a lot of stories, making ourselves sound like badasses. So when push came to shove, and it was time to show if we could steal a car, rob a store, or break into a house—we couldn't. I'm sure we looked more like dumbasses running wild in the street than badasses.

The important thing to understand is *why* foster kids do what they do or say what they say. Imagine being in a situation where everything you said, did, or thought was controlled from the time you were little. You were never allowed to use your imagination freely; you had to ask permission for everything; you were treated like shit from the time you could remember; you received no love and no respect. The only type of attention you knew was that of the negative kind.

Now you leave this environment that is all you have known for years, and for one reason or another, you end up in foster care, where everything is completely different. You're treated with respect, your imagination is appreciated and allowed, and people that are strangers to you are filled with love. They sincerely want to help you. They accept you for who you are and not your behavior because that definitely needs to be changed, but they accept you for what makes you the person that you are. There are rules to abide by, and of course, if you break them, then there are consequences. The rules are realistic, and you don't get beaten if you disobey them.

On top of that, you meet all kinds of foster kids, and right away you try to establish your ground with them. You try to act tough by standing up for yourself, even to the biggest kid, so that nobody bullies you. The stories you tell aren't true, but you try to make others believe you are tough. Once they believe you, you are the leader, and you have followers. This makes you the one in charge and the one with all the control.

The freedom is overwhelming, and it's a lot to take on. This is something you aren't used to, and you don't know how to act. Of course you would never show that to the rest of the foster children. So therefore, running away is a huge act of defiance. You think you can run away from all of your problems, but in actuality, all you're doing is causing more problems for yourself and heading in the wrong direction, which can be dangerous.

CHAPTER FIVE

Escalating Trouble

When I started running away from my second foster home, the cops would always catch me and take me back. After about the third time, they gave me a firm warning that if I did it again, they would take me to a juvenile hall. I didn't take them seriously, and I ran away a few days later. I suffered the consequences. It was my first time being in trouble with the law. I had a lighter in my pocket when they caught me, and when I got to the police station, I was put into a room filled with filing cabinets and other supplies to wait. I took out my lighter, set some of the papers on fire, and then went along the wall with the flames. The wall turned black, and the papers that were on fire were burning the carpet. The officer came back into the room and noticed what I had done. His mouth fell open, and he screamed, "What the hell have you done?" I was laughing hysterically, watching him frantically put out the fire.

After it was out, he stared at the wall and then back at me. It was then that I was transported to juvie. Sarah actually brought Juana to see me while I was there. I was so surprised and happy to see her...my sister, that is. Sarah just there coldly, and they didn't stay long. She didn't let my sister and I really talk either. I told her to bring my sister back to visit me again, and she said she would. Of course that never happened. I was released from juvie after being there for a month, and I was taken back to the mental health facility.

My stay at the facility this time around really took a toll on me. I saw a lot of things, and I was acting out in anger. I saw other kids cutting themselves, trying to hang themselves, and wounds that were self-inflicted. I understood why they did it. I remember the feeling of relief I got as I dug my nails into my hand or clenched my jaw so hard that my teeth hurt. I was going to show them, and when I was done, they would know what I was all about. They were going to suffer my wrath.

It didn't take me long to give up and show my hate for the world and myself. I thought it was awesome to start riots in the unit and call the staff names. I had control of other kids in the unit, and I knew it. Then there were times when I would jump in on the action; when one of the other kids started acting up to the point that they were being restrained, I would charge the staff members that had the kid in a hold. That became very dangerous. Of course at the time, I didn't see it like that. Other staff members would be alerted to the situation unfolding in the unit, and I would pick up the biggest chair and throw it. I made barricades, ran around the unit, and acted like a wild animal.

I remember this one staff member in particular. He was at least six feet tall, and I told him I was going to kick his ass and kill him. He laughed. That really pissed me off. I charged him, teeth bared, fists clenched, and growling loudly. He was ready, and all he had to do was put me into a hold. I would put up a good fight though. About two other staff members would have to assist him in subduing me. Then they would all help take me into a room off the unit; it was called the quiet room.

They would put me in restraints, and I hated that so badly. I said some of the meanest things and screamed forever whenever they did that. I would tell the staff members that whenever I was let out, I was going to kill all of them. Eventually, I would work myself into such a rage that I would be hurting myself from struggling to get out of the restraints. They would have to come back in with the nurse on duty and give me a sedative called Thorazine. I would fight to stay awake. The first time I was given Thorazine I fell asleep quickly, but over time, I built up a tolerance to it. It eventually stopped working as well as the first time.

I had been at the facility for about six months at this point in time. I was getting worse, and I was literally going crazy. It didn't matter how many times I was restrained and strapped down. I was fighting everything and anybody that got in my way.

I was moved from the facility to a mental hospital that was about four hours away. At the new facility, there were a lot more kids, suicide attempts, and therapy groups. The groups were supposed to help us with our issues and teach us how to communicate our feelings, including those about our past. I sincerely tried to get involved, but it seemed like the harder I tried the worse things got. I started taking the end of pencils and cutting myself with them, and I rubbed my arms raw with the erasers. I don't recall the exact amount of time I was at this hospital, but before I knew it, I was being transferred to another one. I was at this facility for quite awhile. Over the years I had become a ward of the state, so they could do whatever they deemed necessary.

The facility had three main cottages named Camino, Ketron, and Orcas. Again, I went through a series of tests. I was eventually put on some medication, and although I don't remember the name of the medication, I do remember having an allergic reaction to a little blue pill I was taking. My head started moving involuntarily, and I couldn't stop grinding my teeth. One of the staff members actually thought I was trying to get attention by doing these things, and he told me to knock it off. I told him I wasn't doing it on purpose and asked if he could please get the nurse. The nurse came out and said, "Oh shit! She's having a reaction to her meds." As soon as everything was under control with my medications, I felt like myself again, but my neck was sore, my jaw hurt, and I was exhausted. I slept deeply that night.

I remained in this facility for about a year. My stay there wasn't easy. I caused hell whenever I could, and my behavior was explosive. I learned to be very conniving and manipulative as well. A lot of the staff became impatient with me, and I knew that they didn't like me. There were three staff members in particular that disliked me, not including the nurse. The nurse tried his best to work with me, but regardless of that, I continued being defiant. I got locked up in the quiet room quite a lot, but the only difference at this facility was that they didn't use restraints. Whenever they would lock me up, I would bang my head on the floor until my forehead was swollen, as well as hit my fists on the walls until they were swollen too. I enjoyed the pain. At the time, I didn't know why I felt like that. Years later, I learned through therapy that it was because I hated myself and my life, and I wanted anyone I crossed paths with to see the pain. There were times I would imagine the banging of my head and hitting the walls was me hurting my adoptive family.

I got pleasure from freaking out one of the female staff members by talking in a satanic way, telling her I was going to get her. She would get so scared that she would take off running towards the office, and I would just laugh hysterically at her. I knew I could freak her out any time I wanted. It felt good having that type of control. I hated adults, so being able to control her by something I would say or do made me feel so powerful.

As I became crueler towards the staff members, I started noticing that not only did I hate them, but that I also hated myself. Whenever they would give me compliments, it usually set me off. I didn't want to be told good things about myself because I didn't believe them, and I was certain that I wasn't a good person. I was cutting myself and praying to Bloody Mary. I remember that I used to turn off all of the lights in the bathroom, repeat "Bloody Mary" several times, and then I would see a dark figure standing behind me. The bathroom would get so cold, and I could sense the evil around me. At the time, I thought I was tough, so I would get other kids involved. If they freaked out, I would shove them out of the bathroom, calling them names. Besides, who cared? God sure didn't. God allowed all the bad things to happen to me. He was no good to me, and I certainly wasn't going to serve him. So I cut him out of my life. I called the kids who got scared stupid, but it was actually me who was the stupid one, turning my back completely on God.

Needless to say, my actions towards others and myself worsened. I cut myself so deep once that I had to get about ten stitches. I was put into the quiet room a few days later, and I ended up pulling all of the stitches out, reopening the cut. The nurse kept on trying to talk to me, but I smeared the window with blood so that he couldn't see me. He kept on calling my name, and I didn't answer. He and another staff member finally came in, and I begged them to let me out. He cleaned up my wrist and told me I would be let out as soon as I was quiet for half an hour. It was past midnight when I was finally let out. I went to bed but started getting restless. I decided to plan my escape with the help of another girl.

CHAPTER SIX

Escape!

One Saturday morning when everybody was doing their chores, we turned on the music, and using utensils we had stolen from the kitchen, we picked at the seal around the window. We laid down a sheet on the floor and tacked a blanket up around the window just in case the glass shattered from all of the pressure. Eventually the window shattered. The glass was still in place behind the blanket, so we had to remove the blanket and quickly pull out all the glass, which had fallen onto the sheet that we had placed on the floor. Then we made our grand escape. We ran so fast down to the fence, jumped it, and we were free!

We ran for quite awhile, and eventually we were able to bum some money in order to take a bus to Seattle. The girl knew some people, and we ended up going to their house. They were junkies and were extremely paranoid while we were there. However, they did feed us, let us take a shower, and change. Afterwards, we left. We really didn't have anywhere to go, so we wandered the streets during the day. We tried asking for rides, but a lot of people didn't trust us. One man actually said, "How do I know you aren't going to stab us and take our money?

Are you crazy? I'm not giving you guys a ride!" That day was hopeless, and we ended up spending the night on the streets.

The next morning we were cold and hungry. I woke up not feeling so well. We tried to find food. Eventually we walked into a store, stole some food, and ran far away from the store to find an area to eat. We went walking afterwards and ended up on some railroad tracks. Nothing but woods surrounded us. We had no clue where we were. We ended up on a beach where a bunch of Asian people were throwing out nets and pulling in oysters. A lady tried to talk to us, but we couldn't understand her.

We went back up into the woods and saw a rough-looking man standing outside of his car. When he saw us, he jumped into his car and began chasing us. We took off running and slid down a few steep hills. This continued for about twenty minutes. Finally, we ended up on some street. I'm sure we were quite a sight. We were dirty and breathing hard. As we walked down the street, we found an old abandoned house and sat down on the porch. Neither of us saying a word, we were both replaying in our minds what had just happened.

I still wasn't feeling well, but I told the girl we had to figure out what we were going to do. We started walking again. We walked forever, and by nightfall, I was feeling dizzy and hot. I wasn't walking straight, and my knee was hurting. I told the girl something was wrong, and eventually I started feeling delirious. We talked about what to do. Finally we came to the decision that I should call the police from a pay phone and turn myself in. She, on the other hand, didn't want to go back, so she hid nearby until the police came for me. I couldn't talk straight to the officer. He probably thought that I had been drinking or was on drugs. I explained the best that I could how I was feeling. I don't remember the car ride, but when I was finally back at the facility, I went straight to bed.

The next morning I woke up feeling worse than I did when I went to bed the night before. I was hallucinating and swore everything around me was moving. Whenever I tried to walk, I would step really high because the floor looked like hills. The nurse wasn't coming in until a little later that morning, and I told one member of the staff on duty that I was feeling weird. I decided to take a shower, and while doing so, I noticed my left knee was swollen. I was having a hard time standing on it in the shower, but I finished up and lay back down. My room felt like it was spinning. I held my head and closed my eyes in an attempt to try and make it stop. I woke up a little later and managed to make it out to where the staff was. Some other staff members had come on duty and told me to sit down while they went and got the nurse.

The nurse came, took my temperature, and said, "Oh shit! Your temp is 105!" I showed him my knee, and I was immediately taken to the hospital. I don't remember everything that happened because I was very sick, but I do remember that I was put on antibiotics. I had an infection in my knee and was in bed for a few days. When I ran away and was at those people's house, I shaved my legs and cut my knee in the process. I put a Band-Aid over it and didn't think much about it. I took off the Band-Aid just before we were chased by that man, and dirt must have gotten into the cut, which later caused the infection. It was a healing process, but eventually I was back to my old self again.

During the time I was at this facility, I was able to go to school, but I struggled with staying in class. I felt anxious all the time and got bored easily. I thought that in order to stay entertained I had to act out. So needless to say, I ditched class a lot. However, I did enjoy one class in particular, and it was a computer class that taught just the basics. I especially liked the speed-reading computer program and the sounds the keys made as I typed. I think the facility did what it could do for me during my stay there, and I fought the system the entire way. However, I don't know that I was any better than when I first arrived there. Regardless, my stay there was terminated after about a year and a few months, and I was placed in a different facility. I was never given a full reason as to why I was moved, but I pretty much figured it was due to my behavior. Each time I was moved from a foster home or facility, I acted on this sense of power I had, and I would challenge and push every rule until I knew they felt defeated. I learned over time they couldn't hit me or do anything to me that would be harmful. I used that to my full advantage.

CHAPTER SEVEN

Locked Up

I was moved to another facility; this was a smaller facility, and the school was upstairs. My stay at this facility was just like all the others. It was just as easy for me to run away, and I wasn't any easier to manage. I stayed at this facility for about eight months. The memories of my adoptive family haunted me daily and worsened as I got older. My hate for them ran deep. I used to draw different severed heads mounted on top of stakes, and I would tell the staff they were the different members of my adoptive family, expressing how much I wished I could kill them.

Emotional breakdowns became a frequent thing for me. At this facility, the staff would hold you and sit with you in a room that was visible to the other staff members, letting you cry or just talk. I tried to open up to them, but then I would become angry. I would start calling one staff member that tried helping me names, and I even tried to hit him. They tried to calm me down, but most of the time I would end up in the quiet room. I tried threatening them, promising I would never talk to them again, and saying that I hated them. I wanted out. I wanted to be free. I felt every move that I made was controlled. I thought

I could do much better on my own. I was fed up and determined to get out of there one way or another. My way of getting out was to be a handful.

First, I made a plan with another kid to burn the facility down. We put papers and other items in a garbage can, lit it on fire, and placed it in the bathroom. If we had actually thought about it, we would have known that the concrete floors and walls weren't going to catch on fire. The only things that would catch fire were the shower curtains. The smoke filled the bathroom, setting off the fire alarms and causing not only an evacuation of the building, but also a huge stir.

The staff had no doubt as to who had set the fire and stopped both of us immediately. The emergency crew showed up, and after about an hour or so, everybody was allowed to go back inside. However, the two of us were isolated from everyone else. It was decided that one of us had to go to juvie. Guess who that lucky one was? Of course, it was me. I didn't know how the decision was made, but I was the only one that went that night. I was locked up for about a month, surrounded by the most popular gangs at that time, the Crips and the Bloods. They all wanted to know what "I claimed," and at first, I was harassed by a guy that was a Blood member. Some of the other female inmates knew I wasn't into any of that, and they stuck up for me. They called me "Crazy." That was my name to them. I didn't talk much, and I talked mostly to myself. At night, I sat up in my bed, rocking back and forth, unable to sleep. That was a long month.

Eventually I was taken back to the facility. As soon as I returned, the staff sat me down and had a serious talk with me. They told me that up until now I was going about things the wrong way, but they were going to give me a second chance. I thought about it and decided to behave myself. I actually went to school and tried to obey the rules. Man, what a challenge that was for me, but I was doing it.

One day, I was surprised by some news I received. I found out that I had two sisters who were adopted by a different family. They were younger than me and were twins. I also learned that my other sister Estela was living with them as well, and she was coming to visit me. I was so confused but excited nonetheless. I was never told about any other sisters of mine, but at that time, I was just excited to have visitors. I wanted it to be perfect. I asked the staff if it was possible for me to buy them something. Somehow the staff gathered up some money for me and took me to the store. The staff member that took me helped me pick out some presents. I was proud of what I got.

Finally the day came for my visit, and I was introduced to my twin sisters, saw Estela, and met their adoptive mom. I gave the twins a white bear that had a red and green scarf, and I gave their mom a beautiful picture. She said that the picture we picked out for her matched perfectly the colors in her living room. I don't recall if I bought anything for Estela, but regardless, it was a nice visit. Although I didn't talk much and spaced out frequently because of the medicine I was on, I felt truly happy, and I wished I could have expressed that better. I'm not sure how long we visited for, but like all good things, it came to an end. As I watched my sister who I had grown up with walk out of the facility, a rush of sadness overcame me, and then the anger took over.

I stayed pretty quiet for next couple of days, but that didn't last long. One day at school I just flipped out. I started running around the class, being disrespectful, and causing all sorts of problems. My teacher had the window that led to the rooftop open, and I crawled out it with some other kids. We began running around on top of the roof. I found it funny because the staff was scared for us, and they kept on yelling at us to get down because we could fall. One staff member actually got on top of the roof with us and was trying to coax us back inside. I would run really close to the edge just to freak him out. They said that if we didn't get back inside, they would have to call the police. A few of the kids listened and went back inside, but five of us found another way off the roof and ran away.

We wandered the streets together for a little bit, and then two of the children went in their own direction. Three of us stuck together. We eventually got hungry and found a store. I wanted some candy but had no way to pay for it, so I stole it. I stuffed my pockets with as much as I could fit. As I walked out, I was chased down by two store managers and caught. The other two children took off running, and I was taken back inside. They told me to empty my pockets, and then they took a picture of me with the stolen items. They banned me from ever returning to the store. Then the police picked me up and took me back to the facility. The following days were hell. I think the staff had given up on me, knowing that they couldn't help me anymore. I was disturbing the treatment of the other patients and being defiant.

I was a few months shy of turning fourteen years old when the foster home that had taken care of Estela wanted to give me another try. They also had a surprise waiting for me. My sister that had been left behind in our original adoptive home, Juana, was there. She was so happy to see me. She had a cast on her arm and was sitting on her bed. I said hi, and we talked for a little bit, catching up. I asked her what happened to her arm, and come to find out, one of the foster kids had done it. My sister had the misconception that I was there to protect her, and that from now on she and I were in this together; nobody was going to mess with her anymore. I let her down in a big way. I turned on her and ran away a day or so later. I left her behind again. For the most part, during the time my sisters and I were in foster care, we were in our own worlds. We had to deal with our own situations by ourselves and in our own way. The sense of family was never instilled in us. When we lived together in our adoptive home, we took care of each other, but outside of that bond, we didn't know the true meaning of family, which was in most part due to the abuse. So I did it again. I left my sister behind and started hanging around with the wrong crowd.

I came into contact with a gang called Florencia 13. I started hanging out with them, and they told me what I had to do if I wanted to join, which I never did. I just followed them around everywhere. I started drinking and smoking, and I even learned to speak Spanish. I thought I was so cool. After my caseworker found out that I was hanging around known gang members, I was moved to a group home about an hour away. It was there that I ran into a girl who was locked up in juvie with me. She instantly remembered me. I recognized her face but couldn't remember where I had seen her before. She reminded me where I knew her from, and it only took about a week before she and I came up with a plan to run away. The staff did their checks the same time every day, and since we knew this, we were able to use it to our advantage. After the last night check, we put our plan into motion and ran away. We went to her friend's house, and I learned quickly learned what it was that they did for a living. That's where I was introduced to marijuana and cocaine.

CHAPTER EIGHT

Is This Love?

The girl introduced me to the family, and we stayed with them for about a week or so. During that time, there wasn't a day that went by that we didn't get high. She was into the drug business, and she knew the ropes. I actually went with her when she sold. I held onto the money and stayed quiet, and she took care of me. She bought me clothes, fed me, and kept me high. Eventually, she got a fake driver's license and bought a car. Once we had the car, we went to a location about forty minutes away. We stayed with different families she knew and partied a lot. Sometimes we would go to play in the arcade and hang out with her sister. Each day was exciting, and I loved my freedom. I thought I had escaped the system. Our regular trips eventually turned my life in a different direction.

During one of our trips to the arcade, there was this one guy in particular that I would always see, and he noticed me as well. My Spanish was broken, so I had a hard time communicating with him. My friend translated for me though. The more time I spent talking to him, the more I liked him, as he did me. One day he told my friend to tell me he wanted me to go home with him, but

I was a little leery. I made it very clear that I wouldn't go unless she went with me. We went to his house and found that it wasn't just him living there. All of his family, including his nieces, nephews, brothers, sister, and even some friends, lived there. The house was old, and the family was very poor. Regardless, I felt comfortable because of his family, and I felt like I had finally found a place I could call...HOME! My friend stayed with us for a few days but eventually decided to leave. She told me she was going to find an apartment, and she would see me later. So there I was alone with this guy and his family.

Right away, I jumped in to help out where ever I could. I was really excited to learn about my culture. I wasted no time in learning how to speak Spanish, cook, and work. The working part was very familiar to me, especially after the farm life I had. His mom cooked everything from scratch, and the food was wonderful. The tortillas were cooked outside by fire on a huge, flat, round piece of thick metal called a "comal"—basically it's a metal hot plate, but this one was big enough to cook about twenty-four tortillas. Her husband made it for her. She washed all the clothes and sheets by hand. Plus, we worked in the fields during the summer. It was the only source of income they had. His mom taught me so much, and my Spanish was getting better every day.

After about six months of being with this guy, I began to notice his controlling personality. He hated when I went out with my friend, and of course, I always came back high. Regardless of that, he didn't want me out at all. He would tell me I was his, and that I couldn't hang out with her anymore. I didn't listen, and that really pissed him off. I came back one evening after being out all day, and he was in the bedroom. I walked in, and he immediately asked me, "Where have you been, bitch?" I told him I had been with my friend. He asked me if I was high, and I got lippy with him, saying, "Maybe! Why do you care?" He slapped me. I was shocked, and I just stared at him. Then he grabbed me by my shoulders and said, "I am so sorry. I love you, but you aren't going out anymore." Little by little, my days of feeling free and hanging out with other people came to an end. Sometimes, if I wanted to be with my friend, I would run away just so I could see her. I would stay gone for a few days, and each time I ended up going back, back to him. I would get slapped around whenever I came back, but he would always reassure me that he was sorry and loved me.

Fourteen went by quickly. Between running away from the group home, getting introduced to drugs, and meeting a guy, the year just flew by. I was young, and no one had ever talked to me about sex. I didn't know what happened when you had unprotected sex. I found that out the hard way, and the result was…I got pregnant. I found out I was pregnant when I was about five months along after talking to my friend about the symptoms I was showing, one of which was a small bulge in my stomach. I was scared.

When I told my boyfriend I was pregnant, he yelled at me, "How am I supposed to take care of this baby?" He suggested that maybe we should go to DSHS (Department of Social and Health Services) for help. I didn't realize at the time the steps that were required in order for us to get help, and my name was in the system as a runaway. So I was put back into a foster home. I was permitted weekend visits to see my boyfriend. That surely would have never happened if they knew that he was hitting me, but I didn't say anything. The months flew by, and before I knew it, I was placed into a foster home that was equipped to take care of teen moms. I was the only teen mom in the home, but my caseworker thought it would be perfect for me. This way the foster mom could spend more one-on-one time with me.

CHAPTER NINE

Teen Mom

April 23, 1990—at the young age of fifteen, I became a mom. The labor was long and hurt badly. I didn't realize what it took to give birth to a child at the time. The doctor that was monitoring my labor was very opinionated about "children having children," as he said it. At first, he wouldn't give me the epidural shot to reduce the pain because he said that it would teach me not to have another baby. My foster mom was all over that one! I don't know what happened, but I never saw that doctor again throughout the rest of my labor. I gave birth to a baby boy. I didn't know the first thing about taking care of a child, much less a baby. All I knew was that he cried a lot, that I wasn't getting any sleep, and that my body hurt. I was very stressed out.

I lasted like that for about three weeks, and I was in tears all the time. My foster mom was supposed to be helping me, but she was gone with her boyfriend most of the time. So I was left all alone to deal with a baby. I'm not sure how, but Sook found out where I was. She called me to see how I was doing. I told her that I didn't know what to do with the baby, and I needed help. She suggested that I try to get a hold of my aunt and uncle who lived about four hours away and maybe they could give me some ideas. My uncle is Roger's brother. I got in touch with them, and eventually a plan was in place for them to come and get me. They were going to help me put my baby up for adoption.

I don't remember how long it had been since I last saw my aunt and uncle, but I know it had to be when I was little, growing up in my adoptive home. So whenever I saw them at the age of fifteen with a baby, it was a little strange at first. At the same time, I was glad to have adults around to help me. When we arrived at their home, my cousins were there and curious to see my baby. They took over right away, bathing him and making sure he was warm and well fed. They also fed me and told me to take some time for myself. All I did was take a long shower and clean up.

My aunt and uncle talked to me about a local adoption agency, and the next day my aunt took me there. We talked to an agent regarding the adoption process. It was a lot of information to take in all at once, but I was very clear with the agent that I didn't want a closed adoption. I wanted my son to know his culture. They had a hard time finding a family that was willing to do an open adoption and that was bilingual. Then they had a hit! There was a couple who couldn't have children. The lady was Mexican, and the man was Caucasian. They were the only couple that came close to meeting my requests. However, the adoption itself was going to be a process, but they were able to take him right away because they were foster parents as well.

I can't even begin to explain the sadness that filled me when I had to turn my little baby boy over to complete strangers. I never met the foster parents, but I was assured that I would be able to get updates on him throughout the years. I was allowed time alone with him one last time, and I cried so hard. I told him that I didn't hate him and that I loved him more than anything, but there was no way I could take care of him. He was just a baby, so he didn't understand what I was saying. I still felt the need to tell him that, even if he didn't understand.

After I gave him to the agent, I just sat there. My aunt came and got me, and she walked me out, crying with me. She tried to comfort me by telling me that I did the right thing, and he would be okay. That night my aunt asked me about the charges I had pressed against Roger. During my stay in one of the facilities, I had told the staff that my adoptive dad had raped me when I was younger and that I wanted to press charges. I went as far as to talk to a detective and had some serious allegations against Roger. I did not care; I just wanted to see him hurt and be in as much pain as I was and had been. She very kindly and lovingly explained how serious the charges were, but on the other hand, she understood why I would want to see Roger get into trouble and possibly end up in prison. I did listen and admitted I had lied, and the next day we contacted my caseworker and told her the charges needed to be dropped. Surprisingly, she didn't ask any questions and said she would contact the detective I had been talking to. After that I didn't hear anything regarding the charges I had tried to press against Roger. That night in bed, for the first time in a long time, I said a prayer, and I prayed for my little boy that night and every night after.

I stayed with my aunt and uncle for a little while, but I was very unhappy. I missed my boyfriend and his family, and I wanted to go see him. They encouraged me to put him in the past. They wanted me to concentrate on myself and my education. I wasn't having that. I didn't want their help anymore, and I was feeling anxious. I wanted to leave. They even tried to become foster parents for me, but I was stubborn and wanted to leave. So my wish was granted. Before I could go, I had to complete a drug treatment program. I went to a treatment facility with a three-month program, but I didn't take the treatment seriously. I actually learned how to huff chemicals. I didn't stay clean, but the staff wasn't aware of this. I graduated from the program, which I couldn't have given two hoots about, and I went to another foster home.

I saw my boyfriend the first chance I got. He asked about the baby, and I told him he was in a foster home waiting to be adopted. He called me all kinds of names, slapping me around, and saying how he wasn't going to allow anyone to adopt his child. I told him he wasn't there when I had the baby, and, as a matter of fact, he wasn't there through the most of the pregnancy. During my pregnancy, he was in jail for drinking and driving! That got his blood boiling, and he slapped me again, calling me more names. Somehow, he talked me into trying to get our son back. I really didn't want to, but he promised so much. I thought it was going to be easy now that he said he would help me take care of the baby. He wanted to be a part of our baby's life.

I did ask for my baby back, and because the process for the adoption still wasn't complete, I was allowed to get him back. I moved into another foster home that was equipped for a teen mom, and my son was brought to me. I kept him for a few months. During the few months I had him, my boyfriend was in and out of jail and only saw our son a few times. He never bought him anything. So there I was again, with our son and without help. He cried a lot. It was almost as if he knew where home was, and it wasn't with me. He wasn't familiar with me at all. My time was spent dealing with the baby, going back and forth with my boyfriend, and going to school.

During all this, I got pregnant again. I wasn't thrilled, but this time I made up my mind that I wasn't giving it up for adoption. My son was back and forth between his foster parents, who were trying to complete the adoption process, and me. I was going to a vocational school for teen moms, and I only had a few more months until I turned eighteen. I had to be moved to another foster home that could accommodate me with my two kids. On April 22, 1992, I gave birth to my daughter.

CHAPTER TEN

Making a Decision

I continued going to school and trying for my GED. That never happened. It fell through because I got sidetracked and quit school after I finished the program in exploring childhood careers. During my time in the program, I learned a lot about parenting and relationships. One of the topics was about domestic violence. I learned that the relationship I was currently in wasn't healthy, and that it could turn into a very dangerous situation for me. I thought about the time my boyfriend whipped me with a belt; when his mom found out, she slapped him around, telling him never to do that again. He also took a speaker and slammed it into my face, leaving the left side of my face swollen and bruised. Lots of memories flooded my mind as I took that class. After a while, my caseworker started to suspect that something was wrong but could never pinpoint what it was. Of course, I never said anything. My visits with my boyfriend were limited, and I was only allowed to see him at the DSHS office.

After having my daughter, I only had a few more weeks until I was eighteen, and I was still very unsettled. I had no way to take care of myself, and if I stayed in the system after turning eighteen, I would be placed in a different home that could help me continue on with my education while assisting me with my children. The only way I could stay in the system was by remaining in school. When I turned eighteen, I wanted nothing more to do with the system. I wanted my freedom. My boyfriend and I were still back and forth, and I really didn't know if I wanted to stay with him anymore. Despite my feelings, I decided to exit the system and live with my boyfriend.

Before I moved in with him, I had some major thinking to do, and that was to decide what to do with my son. Even though he spent time with his father and me, we were always arguing, and he would hit me in front of my little boy. There was actually one time my boyfriend slapped him in the face because he was crying. I shoved him and got up in his face and told him he will never lay a hand on him again.

I was struggling with how to show my child manners and how to respect me. I tried using some of the parenting techniques I learned at parenting classes, but it was so frustrating because he saw his dad hitting me, so he thought he could do the same thing. My boyfriend would show him how to bounce basketballs off my head and how to punch me and tell him to call me "bitch." In the back of my mind, I knew this was no life for my son so I gave him back to the foster home, and I actually met the foster mom. She was very sweet, and I knew she would make a great mom for him. She gave me her number and said that any time I wanted to see him I could. She just wanted to give him a good life. I never did tell her what my son's father had been showing him or that he got slapped by him, but I knew I was doing right for my son.

My boyfriend and his family moved to a trailer court that sat along the highway. I had only been back with him for about a month, and I was still healing from having my daughter. He went to work in the fields with the rest of his family. I was in the kitchen cutting meat and talking to his younger brother. I wasn't much of a cook, but his brother was showing me how to cut and cook the meat. My boyfriend came home from work very hungry one day, saw that the food wasn't ready yet, picked up the pan that I was using to cook the meat, and tossed it onto the counter. He turned towards me, slapped me, called me names, and pushed me into the back room. This time I was fighting back. Damn it, I had had enough!

He threw me onto the bed and was choking me. All I could think was that I better fight. I kicked him in his privates, and he let go of my neck. I got up and punched him in the face. The fight was on! He kicked me in the stomach, and I felt a gush of blood. Then he pushed me out of the door that was connected to the bedroom, and I fell on the ground outside. I got up while he was freaking out and throwing things at me, and I ran around to the front door. I grabbed my daughter, who was sleeping in the front room at the time, and I ran down to the highway.

I was running so fast, and then I felt someone pull my hair. I turned around to see that it was him. He told me to go back to the house with him. I told him, "No! I don't want to be with you anymore." He grabbed my arm, walked me over to a grassy area on the side of the road, and started talking all sweet to me. He apologized for the millionth time, and I kept telling him no. He said, "Well, you are not going to leave with the baby," and he started pulling on her. I held on to her tighter, but I was afraid she was going to get hurt in the struggle, so I let go.

As he took off with the baby, I thought about following him back, but something told me to keep on running, so I did. I ran to a gas station and called my son's foster mom. I explained to her everything that had happened, and she told me to hang tight and that she was on her way. It took her about an hour to show up, and the whole time I was praying that my daughter was safe. Once she arrived, we called the cops. They went to the trailer to arrest him and to get my daughter. When they showed up, my boyfriend's mom was holding onto the baby and told them that he ran off. She had found the baby lying on the bed in the living room all alone in the trailer. I returned to the trailer with my son's foster mom, gathered all of my belongings, and went to stay with her for a few weeks.

The police took pictures of my bruises and took a statement from me. He never served any time for what he did though. In the meantime, I had no one besides my daughter and my son's foster mom. I did stay with her for a little bit, but she told me that I needed to have a place of my own for my daughter and I—that was okay with me! She helped me find a place to live and she was constantly checking in on us, making sure we were okay. I was able to get help from the state. I finally had a place of my own. It was nothing fancy, but it was a start.

The area I lived in wasn't the worst area, but it was close enough to downtown and a few drug houses. One drug house in particular was only about a half a block from me, and I had met the lady through a friend of mine. She would show up at my door and ask me for food stamps or drugs. I had just moved there, so I wasn't sure of where to go for drugs. I would give her food stamps, and she would tell me she would be right back. She would come back with drugs and ask me to get high with her. I, of course, didn't think twice about it and found my way back into the drug scene.

This time was different though because I had my daughter, and I got hooked on crack. I ran into some of the biggest drug dealers, and they would supply it to me as long as I helped sell it. Sometimes I even had to provide shelter for some of their family members. The only time they were allowed at my place was late at night after the landlord went to bed. At first I thought I had everything under control, but the addiction eventually took over. I became desperate for my fixes. When the drug dealers got caught selling, I had no way of getting my fix, so I used my food stamps to buy drugs. I used the money I was supposed to pay rent with to buy drugs as well. Once, I left my daughter with some lady for a week or so while I got high. I abandoned my apartment to stay with a friend whose boyfriend was a drug dealer. We had to break up the marijuana, remove all of the seeds, and put the measured out amounts into baggies. He also sold other types of drugs. We mainly did the running around to sell them. He rewarded us with cocaine. That was my main drug, and I was hooked.

After being gone for about a week or so, I went back to see my daughter. She looked skinny, and she had a huge bruise on her cheek. I asked what happened, and the lady said she fell off the couch. I wasn't too happy, but I was also strung out from the drugs. All I could do was think about drugs. I received word that my son's foster mom was looking for me, and she was very worried.

Eventually she found me. She was furious when she saw my daughter and was upset to see how strung out I was. She slapped me and started crying. She told me how much she cared about me and that I needed to take better care of my daughter. She begged me to call my sister, and she wanted me to go live with her for a while. I wasn't ready for all of that just yet, so I stayed in my apartment for a little longer.

As time passed, my addiction worsened. My ex-boyfriend's family actually went to visit my son, and while they were there, they asked about me. His foster mom let me know and got the okay to tell them where I was. They visited me a few times. One day my ex-boyfriend showed up all by himself. He told me he was moving to Chicago, and he wanted to give me one last chance to change my mind. I was over him, so I told him good luck. I made it clear that I wanted nothing to do with him. He asked if I would walk with him down to the bus station, but I refused. At that point, I think he finally understood that I was truly done with him.

He was gone for good. I continued getting high, and before I knew it, a year had gone by. Time flew so quickly, and my addiction was getting worse. I would go into stores with three ladies I hung out with frequently, and we would steal things. We would walk out of the store with the stolen items only to send two other people back in to return the stolen items. They would return the items for cash, and we used the cash to buy our drugs. It was dangerous because eventually our faces became well known, and people started getting suspicious. We would drive all over the area, hitting different stores with the same scam. We broke into a home that belonged to a friend of one of the ladies and took all sorts of items to give to the drug dealers in exchange for drugs.

I ran into some junkies that were needle users, and they told me that whenever I was ready to use the needle, they would show me. They talked about how much of a rush it was to get high like that. I would watch them, and to me, it didn't seem all that exciting. They would throw up, their eyes would roll back into their heads, and their skin had this yellow color to it. I was scared to touch a needle.

One of the junkies told me that I was different, and I needed to get clean, make something of myself; I had no business on the streets or in the drug world. She was always high when she would tell me these things. I also had drug dealers who refused to sell to me because they felt the same way. One dealer actually said that it wasn't a good life, and if I didn't get off the drugs, I was going to be dead soon. I was beginning to wonder what was happening. What did they see that I didn't? When I looked at myself in the mirror, I saw nothing. I tried not to stand in front of a mirror for too long because I didn't like what I saw.

The lady who was taking care of my son never gave up on me, and she noticed how quickly I was going downhill. She always asked what was holding me back and encouraged me to call my sister. I always told her I would, but I never did. She eventually got the number from me and called my sister to explain to her the situation I was in. After that first phone call, those two were constantly in contact with each other, trying to encourage me to move. My drug habit was taking me nowhere, and I was about to lose my apartment. It had been a little over a year since I left the foster care system, and I wasn't doing well for myself. I knew I was getting tired of this life, and I was scared that each time I got high I was going to die or my daughter could be taken from me. The fear I had when I walked in the middle of the night in knee-high snow to a nearby hotel to get drugs, thinking this is the time I'm going to get raped, or the paranoia that somebody was watching me got to be too much, and I knew I had to make a change. One day I made the choice to move to my sister's place. So I did it. I had finally left my boyfriend, the drugs, and all my so-called "friends" behind, and I moved!

PART THREE
Letting Go

I was nineteen now. Was I finally done with everything? Had I finally overcome years of abuse and self-mutilation? I was now a mother, and I had to make a decision. What did I want to do? What kind of life did I want to live? What did God have in store for me?

CHAPTER ONE

Change

I was now living with Estela. We had so much to talk about. She also had a girl about the same age as my daughter. They were only a few months apart, and they got along great. Both of them were a handful, but they were so full of life. They made it a point to get into trouble together. Regardless, they were kids, and they were happy ones at that. My niece was actually the one who taught my daughter how to walk. They called each other "buddy," which was the cutest name to us. I don't know where they got it from, but buddy it was.

On the other hand, I wasn't interested in getting involved with anybody. I was trying to figure out what I was going to do with my life. My sister didn't want me to take on too much all at once, so she suggested that I stay at home to watch the girls while she went to work. She worked hard and had a nice apartment as a result of that. I agreed to stay at home and take some time for myself. I didn't have much to do for a few months. My sister showed me how to do a few things, and I eventually got the hang of everything. I felt independent, and I had been sober now for two months: no relapses or withdrawals. However, I was still trying to figure out what I wanted to do.

My sister kept on telling me about a friend of hers, Ben, and how he was in the military. She would go on and on about how nice he was and that I should meet him. I told my sister I was interested, but that I just wasn't ready for a relationship. She would let it go for a while, but eventually she would bring it back up again. God bless her! All she wanted was for me to be happy.

Sometime around August she told me about a barbecue that the soldiers were having on base. She had been invited by some of her friends and told me I should come, claiming it would be good for me to get out and meet new people. I was hesitant at first, but I ended up going anyways. I have to admit that day was a blast. It turned my life in a different direction. We showed up at the barbecue, and there was laughter, music, and drinking. Everybody was having fun. She introduced me to some of her friends, including Ben, the soldier she was always telling me about.

When I met him, my heart skipped a beat. I wasn't familiar with that feeling. I felt an attraction to this man right from the start. I was thinking, *What the hell?* He also met my daughter who he liked right away. I watched him from a distance, and our eyes would meet a lot. Then he would act like he was busy. My sister encouraged me to talk to him more, and I eventually did. I heard him speaking Spanish, so I knew he was bilingual. I felt comfortable talking to him...once I got the courage to. He was finishing up cooking, so I just sat down at a picnic table watching him. Several of his friends were flirting with me, but I wanted nothing to do with them. I had already set my eyes on my prize—I knew what I wanted.

The barbecue lasted all day, and I had so much fun. Ben was eventually able to sit and talk to me for a little while. The more I talked to him, the more comfortable I felt with him. My sister was the designated driver, and she had to drive other people home. She asked Ben if he wouldn't mind driving me home, and he told her it wasn't a problem. After cleaning up the picnic area, he took my daughter and me to the waterfront. It was absolutely beautiful. We walked along the water and talked. He asked me about the father of my daughter. I told him he wasn't in the picture, and I was a single mom. It didn't seem to bother him at all. He played with my daughter, and we ended up staying out past dark. He drove us home and asked me what I was doing the next day. I told him I wasn't sure, and he said, "Okay. Well then I will see you tomorrow." I laughed and said, "Yeah, okay. It was nice meeting you." I didn't actually think he would show up the next day.

The next morning around ten o'clock he showed up. I was surprised. I admitted to him that I really didn't think he was going to come back. From then on, we saw each other daily. He also started learning a lot about my past, and he knew I had a lot of things that I had to deal with. He was there when my daughter's dad called, saying that he was coming to see me. I told him that I had found somebody else, and I didn't want anything to do with him. He started yelling at me over the phone, saying, "Your daughter is going to be a bitch just like you and will amount to nothing just like her mom." That really pissed Ben off. He grabbed the phone from me and had a few choice words with him, ending the conversation by telling him never to call again. I never heard from him again.

CHAPTER TWO

A Family of My Own

In the beginning of January 1994, Ben and I talked about living together, and we could just see how things went from there. We moved into an apartment not far from the base. It had two and half bedrooms, one bathroom, a small kitchen, a living room, and another room that was big enough for my daughter to have a TV and her little couch set. We were very proud of our first place together. A lot of our stuff came from the dollar store, and we laughed whenever the utensils would break while trying to cut or eat our food. The pans would burn while we were cooking. Needless to say, we learned quickly that some items needed to be bought at other places and not from the dollar store. We settled in, became a family, and my daughter even started calling him Papi, which is Spanish for daddy. I enjoyed being at home whenever he would come home. By July of 1994, we got married and began our journey as husband and wife.

The first five years were the hardest. After my husband and I got married, things were good, but I wish I had known that my demons would follow me into our marriage. I became verbally abusive and physically violent towards the only person that stood by my side, the one that God had given to me. My husband was a good person and an innocent bystander. I was short-tempered with him, and I felt outraged whenever I saw him. I hated that feeling, and yet, I couldn't control it.

One time I threw my daughter's bike at him, and he threw up his arms in defense to block it from hitting his face. A piece of wire on the bike cut his arm. It was a large cut and fairly deep. He was fuming and trembling. He stitched it up himself and left for a few days. His friend ended up taking him to the hospital to get his arm looked at.

This friend and his wife were a really nice couple who lived on base. They were friends to both of us. The man was also in the military, and this couple helped us the best they knew how on numerous occasions. I don't know if my husband's sister or our friends fully understood exactly what I was dealing with, but every little bit of advice and encouragement helped with this struggle.

I attempted suicide once after being married to Ben for a year. My husband's sister had come to stay with us for a little while. She had two jobs at the time, and my husband was still in the military. One day I decided that I had enough of the counseling, the nightmares, and the flashbacks. I wanted to end it all, so I took a bunch of pills. It didn't take long for me to start feeling like the world was closing in around me. I was having difficulty breathing, my ears were ringing, and my heart was pounding. I thought this was it, and I was prepared to die. God had other plans for me though.

My sister-in-law came home early that day. She usually worked all day long, and when she came walking in, I was shocked. I didn't tell her what was going on right away. I walked into my daughter's room, saw her, looked out the window, and something inside me said that it wasn't my time to go; my family needed me. I walked slowly, holding my head, and I felt like I was going to fall over. I made it to where my sister-in-law was sitting, and I started crying. I told her what I had done. She made me sit down, and things started moving pretty quickly after that.

I remember the ambulance and my husband showing up. It was all such a blur. I was completely out of it by the time I reached the hospital. They had to pump my stomach, and I stayed in the hospital for two days. After that, I was taken to the psychiatric ward for evaluation. I stayed there for twenty-four hours. I was diagnosed with Post-Traumatic Stress Disorder (PTSD), anxiety, and battered women syndrome and childhood trauma. I didn't want to take any medications for it. I just wanted to fight this battle on my own. I continued the counseling, and with the help of my husband and God, we were in this for the long haul.

I prayed nightly for God to heal me and to take away the dark shadows that haunted me. The nightmares were horrible, and I hated falling asleep. I dreamed that Roger's face was the moon, and he was watching me all the time.

I also dreamed that my ex-boyfriend was climbing up the side of a wall to get me, and the dream I used to have while I lived with my adoptive family, the one with the boulder that chased me, was back. I felt crazy. I felt like I was in all those bad situations all over again. I had to fight those feelings and memories and remind myself where I was and who I was with.

My husband and I thought maybe I was getting bored, and I had too much time to think about my past. So I got my first job at Subway. I was so proud of that job, and I worked hard. The people that worked there, however, were very cliquish. The thing about being married to a military man is that you are judged on your husband's rank. If your husband wasn't at a rank as high as the other wives' husbands, then they wouldn't associate with you. It may sound strange, but it's true. I told my husband what was going on, and that I thought maybe I should find another job. Well, I guess I got my answer sooner than expected.

I went to work one day and was called into the office. I was asked about sixty dollars that was missing. I told the manager that I had no clue what she was talking about. She fired me and told me I could pick up my final paycheck later that week. When I went back to get my paycheck, the manager apologized, explaining that the missing money was found, and she offered me my job back. I told her I appreciated her apology, but I would never work for her again. I found other jobs over the years and even attempted going back to school several times to get my GED. Regardless of my attempts, I just couldn't focus enough to finish it.

That same month, I found out I was pregnant. We both were very excited, and we started preparing for a baby. Then, two months later, I had a miscarriage, and we both were so sad that we cried in each other's arms for a while. Two weeks had passed, and I continued feeling sick and tired. I told my husband I wasn't feeling right, and I needed to see my doctor. The doctor ran the usual tests: blood drawn, a urine test, and an ultrasound. The ultrasound was because of the miscarriage I had. Before we left the office, my doctor told me I was pregnant. I told him that was impossible because I had a miscarriage. He showed us the test results and said the only thing he could think of was that I was pregnant with twins and had lost one. My husband and I were so excited...still saddened by the one we lost, but excited that we were still having a baby. In October of 1995, we had a beautiful, healthy girl.

CHAPTER THREE

Leaving It All Behind

We had been married for two years now and had two daughters. In 1996, we had an opportunity to leave Washington and go to Japan. I couldn't believe it. My husband was sent to Japan first, but before he left, we found out I was pregnant again. Either way, we made it to Japan a few months after he did. Japan was a neat place, beautiful as well. When I got on that plane to Japan, I had so many mixed emotions; I was finally leaving Washington. I sat with my two daughters, and as the plane took off and ascended higher, looking out the window, tears started trickling down my cheeks. I didn't sob uncontrollably, but I couldn't stop the tears from coming. I think it was at least thirty minutes before they finally stopped. I thought that all my years of struggles and hardships had truly come to an end. So many memories of my life flashed before my eyes.

CHAPTER FOUR

Family Adventures

U nfortunately, our stay in Japan was not very long. My husband had some family matters come up, and we had to leave Japan for Idaho. During our time in Japan, our baby was born in February of 1997. All five of us ended up living in Idaho for about three years. We also added another child to the family in March of 1999, so we had a family of six. That was good enough. Even if I had wanted another baby, I couldn't have one because my last pregnancy was high risk, and our newborn daughter almost died. We counted our blessings and quit adding to our family. We shifted our focus to raising the ones we had.

Regardless of our new location in Idaho and my own family to occupy my time, I couldn't shake the dreams, thoughts, and rage. I was no longer going to counseling, and we were beginning to wonder if our marriage was going to last. We decided that it would be best if we took a break from each other. When I still lived in Washington, my sister Juana had told me she was back in contact with Roger. She had told me that he had changed and was remarried to a wonderful Christian lady. We had visited them on various occasions since then. So during our break from each other, that is where I went to stay. I stayed for about three weeks to clear my mind so that I could fix my marriage. My life had changed in many different areas, one being my heart. I had started seeking God and going to church. I had to learn over time how to forgive and get rid of that hate. I knew for me that I had to give that second chance to Roger, and I, at the same time, wanted some answers. So I tried to build a relationship with him knowing that part of the problem in my marriage was due to my childhood and I had to confront it somehow.

Over those three weeks, Roger read to me from the Bible and prayed with me. I didn't tell him everything, but I did confront him about the way he had treated us when we were little. I asked him why? He blamed a lot of what happened on Sarah, and he also told me that I was too young when everything happened to remember anything, which was total bullshit. I knew exactly what he did to us, and what we went through. I wasn't making up stories. His wife even defended him by saying that things weren't that bad for us growing up. It was too much to bear, and I had to leave. I talked things over with my husband, and we decided that we had taken enough time away from each other. It was time for us to be together as a family again.

When I returned home to Idaho, we got involved in a church, and I prayed for God to intervene, starting with my dreams. For the next year, things were rocky, but we kept our marriage together. Then in 2000, my husband was offered a job in Colorado. He went first to settle in and get trained. We weren't quite sure if all of us were going to move there, or if he was just going to stay there, traveling back and forth to visit us. As the months passed, I couldn't stand us being separated like that. We discussed it, and we all moved to Colorado—Colorful Colorado. It was beautiful. We lived there for about ten years. My dreams followed me there as well, and I continued to pray for an intervention. God answered my prayers.

CHAPTER FIVE

Let God

Since the day I got married, I dreaded going to sleep. Every night was a battle to stay awake; staying awake was the only way to keep the dreams away. I knew I would eventually lose the battle and fall asleep. I also knew that my dreams would be horrible. I relived everything all over again in my dreams. Not only did I relive my past in my dreams, but I would also wake up sweating, angry, and discouraged with God. One particular night I fell asleep quickly and I dreamed about my ex-boyfriend. Except this time I was in Kmart, and he had actually come into the store. Upon seeing me, he came at me, but I felt no fear. I was standing at the exit door, and he was in a little kid's pool, trying to come after me. Regardless of how hard he tried, he couldn't reach me. He was shouting profanity at me and threatening me. I told him he had done enough, and I was married and happy; if he really loved me, he would have never treated me the way he did. In my dream, my husband put his arms around me, telling me it was time to go. I continued looking back through the windows of the store, and I saw my ex still struggling to get out of the pool and run after me. He was just running in circles as we left to go home.

I woke up the next morning, and after having this dream, I knew something was different this time. Other dreams from my childhood seemed to take different forms as well and eventually subsided. As the nights went on, I wasn't having the nightmare anymore. I put two and two together...*God had freed me!* I was able to say what I needed to say through my dream to my ex and to all the people that had hurt me. Now I was in control, and I knew I had a higher power working for me. God was on my side, and he was powerful—more powerful than the devil. The devil had control of me for so long, causing me to do evil and wrong, but God wasn't going to let me become a child of the devil. He had other plans for me, and he was laying it all out right in front of me. All I needed to do was want it.

The next situation I had to face was with Roger. My husband and I talked countless hours about the relationship I had with him, and I prayed constantly. The relationship with him was rocky. I can't say I was ever comfortable around him, and I definitely didn't trust him around my kids. I would see that same cold look in his eyes when he was with my children. The same look he had when I was little. We never allowed the children to stay with him overnight unless I or my husband was present. From the beginning, when I was told that Roger was seeking a relationship with me and my sisters, I put up a wall. I was very cautious and certainly not trusting. However, I did try to accept the idea that maybe he had changed, but in the back of my mind, I remained aware.

When I first saw Roger, he looked happy, and he was actually trying to make up for lost time. The first Christmas we had together when I lived in Washington was crazy. They bought each of us numerous gifts. I felt like a little kid. It was actually fun. We tried to visit as often as we could when we lived in Washington, but when we went to Japan, I didn't have much contact with him. Then, when we lived in Idaho, I would fly back and forth to see him. Regardless of how many times we tried to talk to Roger about the past, he would always have the same response: "It wasn't me. I never wanted to hurt you girls. It was your mom. She made me. You, Mari, were too young to remember anything." It was a no-win situation. For myself, I had to forgive. I knew the memories would always be there, but I also knew I couldn't reach for something that wasn't there. My husband would tell me that I had to quit being "the victim." The fact that Roger was and always will be in denial made it difficult. I didn't like being told that, but it all was true. I had to take a stand, and I quit talking to my adoptive dad.

That was hard for my sisters and me to deal with. We were saddened that it didn't work out. I can only speak for myself, but I was angry. I wondered why he wanted to have a renewed relationship if he couldn't be honest about the past. Each one of us dealt with this differently. For me, I prayed that God would be with him, but at the same time, help me to move on with my family. I couldn't live in a fantasy world. That would destroy me. My husband helped me so much to get over this hump, and over time, it has gotten easier. I love my adoptive dad very much, and I always keep him in my prayers. It still saddens me though. Juana actually hears from him every now and then, but we aren't sure what he is up to now.

As for me, my dreams and rage came to an end. I certainly know my husband is happy about that, as well. I eventually got my GED, and that was a challenge. My jobs over the years have led me in different directions. I worked in a group home, a school for the physically and mentally challenged, a facility for troubled youth, and a correctional facility for men and women. You never know who is actually listening to you, and I always ask myself, "Will these people ever quit using the excuse of how they grew up and always being the victim? Will they ever know what true love is, and allow themselves to be loved?"

Estela, Juana, and myself were reunited with our biological family in Colombia by phone in 2008. That was a miracle in itself. My oldest biological brother had bypass surgery. A missionary couple that lives in Colombia heard about it and went to see him in the hospital. One way or another, they were able to track us down in the States and contact each of us. I have learned so much about where we came from. My biological father actually tried to keep in touch with us while we were living at our adoptive home, but our adoptive parents wouldn't allow it. They never gave us anything he sent for us. He lived until 1984. When I heard that, I was angry that our adoptive parents kept that from us because of jealousy and the hate they had for us. My birth name was Mari Neli Bejarano. Our birth mother loved us and worked very hard for her family.

The summer of 2012, I went to Colombia for a family reunion. I went with my husband, my sister Estela, and her husband. There's not enough words to explain my trip. The minute the plane landed in Colombia, I felt like I was finally home! I got more anxious as we got closer to where my family was standing outside. I wanted to run right to them, but I had to go through Immigration first. All my brothers and sisters along with cousins, aunts, and uncles were standing with a "Welcome to Colombia" sign. We cried, hugged, and kissed each other. They had rented a bus, and we drove back to my brother's house for a feast and to talk.

During our two-week visit, we did a lot of sight-seeing and met some more family. They made it so special for us; they killed a cow and cooked the meat around a fire on big sticks. The meat was delicious—my brothers and sisters are wonderful cooks, and they make all their food from scratch. They had a huge dance, and the party lasted into the next day. They showed us pictures of my biological parents and my sister that died. They say I look a lot like my mom. I learned that even though we weren't raised around them, we all have the same laugh, and the love between us is so strong.

One night, we sat around talking about what happened to each of us after we were adopted. We all had a story to tell; my family in Colombia have suffered and gone through a lot themselves, so we could understand each other's pain. They apologized for not taking care of us, and they felt like they were at fault for what happened with my adopted family. Estela and I told them it was not their fault and to not carry that guilt.

The day came for us to leave—that was so hard. We cried again, hugged, and kissed; none of us wanted to look back to wave good-bye. Though we still keep in touch, I am praying I can return again soon to my brothers and sisters and to my beautiful country...Colombia!

Although we are older, my sisters and I are not that close, not like sisters should be. Our rock is our spouses and our immediate family. We are at different levels of healing and just trying to survive like any other survivor would one day at a time. Unfortunately, our sister Sook, who was adopted from Korea, has separated herself from us going on six years now. I pray for her and hope all is well. The relationship the four of us had growing up will never be forgotten, and we did what we had to do to survive.

Every day I wake up I am thankful for where I am in my life now. Nothing is ever perfect, and I don't know that anybody's life is. We've all had our own struggles. Still to this day, I suffer from PTSD, anxiety, back problems, and my handwriting hasn't gotten any better. I have received comments about my writing, such as: "You write like a little child." I used to get angry about it, but over time I have realized that people don't know my life story or why I write the way I do. So now I laugh and make jokes about it. I receive good responses to that approach.

Most people say they actually like it because it's so clear, and they have no trouble reading it. Regardless of the challenges I face daily, through God's grace and his everyday nurturing love, I can wake up praying:

Okay, Lord. It's another day, and I need you today. I ask that you will take anything that wants to harm me or my family and destroy it. Stand in the way of Satan as he tries to make me regress, or as he tries to shift my thoughts. Thank you, God, for all you have healed, done, and continue to do. You are an amazing God!

I have learned throughout the years how to be a mother and have apologized several times to my girls for being short-tempered. I have learned to deal with marital situations appropriately and not with anger. I have accepted that life isn't easy, and that regardless of what statistics may say, I don't have to be a victim. I don't have to repeat my adoptive parents' mistakes. I can break the cycle of abuse. I have taken a stand and learned to hold my head up high. I know that I can be free...*I broke the chain!*

AFTERWORD

This book was not easy to write. I know I will be criticized. Some people may quit talking to me or wonder why I would want to write about this, but, like my pastor said, "God is in the business of recycling our pain and using it for somebody else's gain." I will tell you the devil has tried to sidetrack me so many times. I have felt the spiritual battle God and Satan are having, but you know what...God again has won!

For all of us survivors who have survived or are still victims of abuse. It only takes one person to believe in you and show you that you are worth being loved. For me, it was my angels that God sent: my husband and four little lives that taught me how to live, love, and laugh. We can't continue to allow the abusers to be our future. We have to fight and show ourselves we are worth being loved, and we don't have to continue being the victim. A lot of us that have been through these types of situations get very angry with God and people. I hated white people, and hate was huge in my heart. I do remember thinking, God, you say you love us and would never leave us, but why did you allow such detestable things to happen. It's fair to say I hated God. As time went on and I started cleaning up my actions and life, I realized and learned that God does not give us more than what we can handle. He does not force people to do evil...people choose that. I didn't ask to be put in that situation and bear no fault in other people's actions, but I am at fault if I continue to follow the same path and choose to do bad to my children or other people. We are all responsible for our actions and can't continue to blame our past. God bless the readers, especially the ones who can relate. This life is only temporary. You can make a difference. I did...I broke the chain!

ABOUT THE AUTHOR

M ari Neli Bejarano Beltran is married with four daughters and is soon to be a first-time grandma. She is currently a certified caregiver working through agencies and privately; she received her CNA in 2013. With a passion for helping others, she devoted two years of her life to working for a severe-needs group home for adults in Idaho. After moving to Colorado, she began working as a paraprofessional for severe-needs children at a local public school. Having been a patient at a mental health facility as a child, Mari always hoped that she could one day give back, using her own personal experience to help children in need. After leaving the public school system, Mari took a job as a childcare counselor for troubled youths at the Emily Griffith Center, which is a non-profit mental health facility. Upon the facility's closing, she worked at a community correctional facility as an officer. After moving to Georgia, even though Mari enjoyed helping others, she decided to take a break and focus on her and her family, specifically, raising her four lovely daughters.

While caring for her family, Mari found the time to finally tell her harrowing story of surviving an abusive home. At the age of forty, Mari published her first book, *I Broke the Chain*. First-time author Mari Neli Bejarano Beltran plans to reach out to children and people all over the world through her own personal experience. She is currently writing letters to all the facilities that helped her throughout her teenage years in hopes of being able to reach out to those who feel like no one cares or understands what they are going through.